D1714905

# Sleep
## The Mysterious Third of Your Life

# Sleep
## The Mysterious Third of Your Life

*Jonathan and Marianna Kastner*

Illustrated by Don Madden

*Harcourt, Brace & World, Inc., New York*

Curriculum-Related Books, selected and edited by
the School Department of Harcourt, Brace & World,
are titles of general interest for individual reading.

Library of Congress Catalog Card Number: 67-22392
Printed in the United States of America

The authors acknowledge their gratitude to Dr. Michael L. Glenn, who served as consultant for this book. Dr. Glenn is a psychiatrist, practicing in New York City, who did research in sleep while he was a student at Columbia University College of Physicians and Surgeons.

# Contents

I    The Patterns of Sleep                    3

II   Dreaming                                20

III  A Different Kind of Sleep               41

IV   Why Do We Sleep?                        61

V    When People Go Without Sleep            82

VI   The Frontiers of Research on Sleep     100

Sleep
The Mysterious Third of Your Life

# I
## The Patterns of Sleep

Each night at bedtime your body readies itself for sleep. Your temperature begins to fall, your muscles relax, the amount of sugar carried in your blood decreases, and your breathing slows. Soon your rate of breathing becomes so slow that it cannot supply enough oxygen, and you begin to yawn. If you want to stay awake, continued yawning will give you the oxygen your body needs.

Soon you go to bed. Seven or eight hours later you

awaken. You have spent one third of your day asleep, yet you probably could not describe your experiences during this time, except for the memory of a dream or two.

Sleep is necessary. Everyone knows that. But few people know how we sleep. And no one knows exactly why. It was not until recently that anyone began to study sleep in a scientific manner. What the first researchers found amazed the scientific world. They discovered that what we call sleep is actually just a name for a number of totally different states, which themselves are almost as different as night and day.

After laboratory researchers had established the basic pattern of sleep in a number of individuals, they set out to learn what happens when people are deprived of sleep. Such an experiment, they reasoned, might teach them why people need sleep. They soon found that there was great danger in going without sleep for long periods of time. Both the bodies and the minds of sleep-deprived volunteers rebelled. After several days the subjects became ill-tempered and experienced hallucinations. Some of them seemed on the verge of nervous breakdowns.

Although very few people set out to stay awake just for the sake of not sleeping, the effects of sleep deprivation are very real to a great many people who may not realize it. Every day thousands of people upset their sleeping and waking schedules by traveling in airplanes. A trip from New York to Chicago adds one hour to a traveler's day, because it is an hour earlier in Chicago than it is in New York. Most people suffer no ill effects from a journey as short as this. Flying from New York to San Francisco, however, can produce a profoundly upsetting effect on the traveler. A person who leaves New York at noon will arrive in San Francisco five and a half hours later. But because of the three-hour time difference between the two cities, it will be only two-thirty in San Francisco. Therefore the length of the traveler's day will be increased by three hours. Although he may have no difficulty in actually remaining awake for three extra hours, his body will begin preparing for sleep at the time it normally would—three hours too early on San Francisco time. His body temperature gets lower, his muscles relax, and his blood sugar drops. By the time he goes to bed, let us say at ten, he is probably so tired that he falls asleep immediately. And sure enough, at five o'clock the next morning he wakes up, because his body is accustomed to arising at eight o'clock New York time. It may take several days before his body completely adapts to the new schedule.

This jet-age problem has come to the attention of almost every traveler. But the men who most frequently feel the effect of changing time zones are the airplane pilots themselves. New York to San Francisco is only a hop, skip, and jump to an experienced jet pilot. What about the man who guides a plane from New York to Rome, eight hours flying time and six time zones away? If he takes off at six in the evening, he will arrive in Rome at 2 A.M. New York time. When he lands, however, Rome time will be 8 A.M. The pilot is faced with the choice of sleeping through the day or trying to stay awake another twelve or fourteen hours until nightfall and then going to sleep. If he decides to stay awake, he will be out of phase with his body. His body will continue to shut down and start up on New York time regardless of his decision. Because of this problem, pilots often stay on their home-city time wherever they go.

Not only pilots and vacationers suffer the effects of rapid changes in time zones. So do busy executives, who may be flying long distances to attend important meetings. Tests have shown that people who travel far and fast cannot make the kind of quick decisions required of an executive or a pilot. In experiments conducted to test the mental capacities of people who have taken trips of this kind, bright people who ordinarily could do complicated mathematical problems were unable to solve them after such a journey. Of course the same thing would occur if the people had been given the problems at or after their normal bedtime. But the tests pointed out that long air trips have the same effect on people as staying up late. This "jet-age fatigue" does not affect travelers who fly from north to south, because such flights do not cross time zones. If a plane from New York landed in South America at nightfall, it would be nightfall in New York, too.

Jet-age travel illustrates only one example of the body's need for a regular day-night cycle. Another example of this need is found in offices where employees switch from day work to night work every week or even every month. Their efficiency is impaired and their work is likely to suffer, for it takes a person from seven to fourteen days to adjust to such a change in schedule.

To study the effects of changing an individual's sleep patterns, a scientist named Nathaniel Kleitman devised a schedule even more disrupting than the ones experienced by pilots and night workers: he increased the length of the normal twenty-four-hour day. First, in order to see what would happen if he escaped from ordinary day and night, he took an assistant and went underground, into a cave far beneath the surface of the earth. There he set up housekeeping. The only light available was the battery-powered light he had brought with him. Therefore, "sunrise" and "sunset" depended on when he turned his light on and off. This way he could live a twenty-eight-hour "day," with fourteen hours of light and fourteen hours of darkness. His assistant managed to adapt; gradually his body began to turn itself on and shut itself off every fourteen hours on the new schedule instead of the sixteen hours on and eight hours off of a normal day. But Dr. Kleitman was so regulated that his body continued on the twenty-four-hour schedule. Although he acted outwardly as though a day was twenty-eight hours long, his body was awake when he was lying down and asleep when the new schedule called for waking. What do these two reactions add up to? Through experiments such as these, scientists have discovered that it is not just the twenty-four-hour cycle of light and dark that determine when we sleep. Nor

is it just habit that keeps us on a twenty-four hour day. The forces that tell us when to sleep and when to wake up are very strong. It now appears that everyone is born with pre-set patterns and that man is not the only creature to have them. It seems as though every living thing is governed by them. Because these forces are so carefully scheduled, scientists call them "biological clocks."

It would be easy to believe that sleep takes place at night because it is dark and that people and animals —and even some plants—awaken with the daylight simply because it is easier to go about daily tasks when the sun is up. This does seem like a reasonable idea. Or does it? It could be the answer for many living things on earth but not for all. To understand why, you must remember one thing about the earth's position in the sky: it is tilted. That tilt is the reason for the changing seasons. When the northern half of our planet is tilted toward the sun, it is summer in the United States. When it is tilted away from the sun, it is winter. Why is this important? Because the length of days and nights changes; nights in wintertime are longer (about four hours longer in the United States) than in summer. But do you sleep longer during the winter months than you do in summer? On dark, cold winter mornings you might wish you could, but most people sleep no longer in winter than they do in summer.

For an even better example, consider the Eskimos, who live in the far north, in Alaska and northern Canada. In their winter the sun is up for only a very few hours, and for a few days in midwinter it does not rise at all. On the other hand, the Eskimos' summer days are much, much longer than ours. And just as there are winter days with no sun, there are summer days when the sun does not set. Yet despite very long days or nights, Eskimos sleep just about as long every day as you do, and at just about the same time.

If it is not just darkness and light that determine when we sleep and for how long, what reason can we find for our daily patterns? As we said before, the patterns do not apply only to people. Birds tuck their heads under their wings and sleep; clams and lobsters are still. Even fish stop swimming, and some tropical varieties settle near the bottom for the night. The bright reds, greens, and yellows that make them so beautiful by day are dimmed in sleep. There are flowers, such as the morning glory, that open and close their blossoms in a regular pattern, too. In England, in olden days when clocks were very rare and not so accurate, some wealthy people had gardens with each kind of flower either opening or closing every hour. Imagine a whole garden for a clock!

It seems as though the entire living world is governed by the mysterious forces known as biological clocks. These clocks do not just regulate what living things do day by day; there are some that control activities that take place just once a year! For instance, the migration of birds and animals is timed by just such a yearly clock. And there is one kind of fish, called the grunion, which slithers out of the ocean to lay its eggs on damp beaches only on the first nights following either the first full moon or the first new moon in March. Every spring, without fail, grunions return to the beaches to lay their eggs.

Another example of carefully timed, once-a-year occurrences is hibernation, the long winter sleep of some animals. One such animal is the ground squirrel. Each autumn the squirrel stores away extra energy in the form of fat by eating much more heavily than usual. As cold weather approaches, it crawls into its den, plump and sleepy. When it emerges in spring it is much thinner and very, very hungry. During the winter months its extra fat was used for nourishment. But a ground squirrel's small body could not possibly store enough fat to keep it alive all winter unless the activities of its body changed. One important change is the lowering of the body temperature. From a normal of about 100 degrees Fahrenheit (normal for human beings is between 98 and 99 degrees F.) it drops to almost freezing. Its heartbeat and rate of breathing also slow down—from about 250 heartbeats a minute to fewer than 10 beats a minute, and from about 200 breaths a minute to 3 or 4. In this slowed-down state the squirrel requires far less nourishment during hibernation than it does during its months of wakefulness. And every phase of hibernation—the extra eating in the fall, the urge to sleep, and the slowing of the body—is dictated by biological clocks.

We now know how important a regular schedule is to every kind of life. We know that not only sleep but also many other activities are controlled by clocks within us. So far, despite all their work, scientists have been unable to find out just what makes these clocks work. But every day (or should we say every night?) more and more is being found out about the effect that clocks have on us. Complicated electronic machines aid scientists in this kind of study. One of the most important of these machines has the long name of electroencephalograph. We might as well abbreviate the name in the same way as the men who use it: EEG. But first let us look into that long name and see if it tells anything about how the machine works and what it does. The first part, *electro,* is not hard to figure out. The machine measures electricity. The middle, *encephalo,* is part of a Greek word meaning "brain." And the last part, *graph,* is derived from another Greek word that means "write." Now we know that the machine measures electric activity (electro) in the brain (encephalo) and traces the patterns of this activity—writes (graph) with automatic pens. Let us see exactly how the machine helps study sleep.

The EEG is used in what are called sleep laboratories. These laboratories are not at all like the ones chemists use. There are no long rows of work benches with test tubes and bubbling vats. A sleep laboratory has at least one bedroom and a control room. In the control room is the EEG. The bedroom may be very much like any other bedroom, but with one important difference. A group of wires is attached to the head of the bed; they lead to the EEG. On the ends of the wires are small disks that act like very sensitive microphones. When they are taped onto a person's head, they can receive the tiny amounts of electricity that are produced in the sleeper's brain. The wires carry this small electric current into the EEG, which acts like the amplifier of a hi-fi set. The EEG turns the small current into larger amounts of electricity. But unlike a hi-fi, the EEG has no loudspeaker. Instead, the current is used to operate the pens that trace the lines on the graph paper. And these are the lines that tell so much about sleep.

Let's start from the beginning, with an example of a typical person in a typical sleep laboratory. When he arrives, he prepares for bed. Then the wires are taped to his head. Some are placed near his eyes, to detect the electricity generated as the eye muscles move his eyes. Others are placed on his forehead, on the sides of his head, and near his ears. There may also be wires that carry messages about blood pressure, temperature, and heartbeat to the machine. So far this may seem as though the EEG is some sort of torture machine, but it is not that at all. The wires do not carry enough electricity to light even a flashlight bulb, and the small amount of current that does pass through them runs from the person into the EEG, not vice versa. Soon the subject is asleep, and the experimenter is settled in his chair in front of the EEG so he can watch the pens tracing their lines on the graph paper. The paper is on rollers and moves past the pens at a steady rate.

The first part of sleep is one almost everyone is aware of. It is the comfortable relaxation of those first few minutes in bed. Some people doze, then awaken, only to doze again quickly. This is known as the threshold of sleep. It is very light sleep; if the subject were awakened during the threshold period, he might not even be aware that he was beginning to sleep. But after a few minutes, if he is undisturbed, the sleeper moves on into the first true sleep, called Stage 1. During Stage 1 the sleeper's temperature begins to fall at a steady rate; his muscles relax, and his heartbeat slows. The pens that register brain waves trace out an irregular pattern, for the sleeper is probably thinking disconnected thoughts that are not really dreams, but more like fantasies or daydreams. Soon some of the pens on the EEG begin to move so fast that they make a chattering sound. Those that register eye movements

have been fairly still, but now they begin to trace wavy lines that indicate that the sleeper's eyes are rolling slowly behind his closed eyelids. The brain-wave line becomes more irregular, with occasional large peaks and valleys. The sleeper has entered Stage 2. Even if his eyes were open he would not see unless a bright light were flashed. (In fact, experiments have shown that people can fall asleep even when their eyes are taped open. The part of the brain that records what the eyes see shuts itself off in sleep, and just as it takes a fairly loud noise to wake a sleeper, only a bright flash of light will disturb him.)

After about forty-five minutes the sleeper enters Stage 3, a part of sleep deeper than Stage 2. His temperature is still falling; so is his blood pressure. The brain-wave line becomes more even, with large, regular waves. The eye-movement lines become almost straight again. About an hour has passed since the subject first closed his eyes, and he is about to enter the deepest sleep, known as Stage 4. During Stage 4 it is extremely hard to awaken him. His brain may hear sounds, but most sounds do not register on his conscious mind. Only a very loud noise will affect his sleep. Sometimes people mutter or actually talk during Stage 4; people who tend to sleepwalk do so in Stage 4. But despite this activity, the sleeper has not yet begun to dream, although his first dream of the night is not far off.

After ninety minutes have passed, the experimenter notices a change in the pattern the EEG pens are tracing. The sleeper is reentering Stage 3. Soon he is back in Stage 2, then Stage 1. But although the brain patterns show the sleeper to be in Stage 1 sleep, his condition is actually much different from the Stage 1 he entered just after he went to bed. Although it is not the restful sleep of Stage 4, it takes the sleeper further from the waking world than he has yet been. He begins to toss and turn, as though he were awake.

In fact, the first sleep experimenters thought their subjects *were* awake. They were mistaken, for this is the dreaming time, when the pens that record eye movements really begin their work. They wag from side to side as the sleeper's eyes move rapidly, as if following the action of his dream. The sleeper's neck muscles have become completely slack, but his arms and legs are tense and often twitch. But the real action is taking place inside the body. The heart has begun to beat wildly and the blood pressure jumps up and down, just as would happen if the subject were awake and in a frightening situation. But strangely, these changes do not necessarily mean that the sleeper is having a nightmare. He may be having a perfectly happy, calm dream.

Because it is the eyes that are the first to indicate this dreaming stage of sleep, the stage is called Rapid Eye Movement, or REM, sleep. It is the only part of sleep during which it is definitely known that dreaming occurs. The first period of REM sleep is short, perhaps only ten minutes. When it is over, the sleeper begins again to go through the four stages of sleep: from Stage 1 he passes into Stage 2, then Stage 3, and Stage 4. And just as happened earlier, he again slips backward until, another ninety minutes later, he is dreaming again in REM sleep.

Although the actual length of time for each stage of sleep varies from person to person, this ninety-minute cycle is the most common. Since most people sleep for seven or eight hours, the various stages of sleep, including dreaming sleep, occur four or five times during the night. And each time the pens of the EEG trace the familiar patterns, signaling the change from one stage to the next.

As morning approaches, the sleeper's body begins to prepare itself for wakefulness. His temperature begins to rise again as does his blood pressure. He awakens after what has probably been a good night's sleep. Most people who take part in the study of sleep are not troubled by the strange surroundings or even by the wires taped to their heads. But a few are. Occasionally a sleep subject will toss and turn the whole night, never quite able to cross the border between wakefulness and sleep. One subject, who was afraid he might have that trouble, decided to read himself to sleep. He settled into bed with the only book he could find in the laboratory—a book about sleep—and was soon fast asleep.

In many experiments the tester will awaken the subject after a few minutes of REM sleep to ask him what he was dreaming. One man, who was obviously a little nervous about being a subject, but not so nervous that he could not sleep, awakened the next morning feeling guilty because he had had no dreams during the night. As he drank his morning orange juice, thoughtfully provided by the laboratory, he apologized to the experimenter for not dreaming. Just as he was getting up

to leave, a buzzer rang. It was the tester waking him to ask him what his dream was about. The nervous sleeper had dreamed the entire incident.

But dreams or no dreams, nervous or calm, when morning comes, the night's experiment is over. In the control room the EEG has been turned off; the pens are still. Two fifths of a mile of graph paper have unrolled past the pens, two fifths of a mile of the tracings of one night of one person's sleep. Now someone must look over the entire roll to see if there is anything unusual, something that might lead to a new discovery about sleep.

# II
## Dreaming

Dreams are familiar to nearly everyone. They have been described by every group of people that has ever existed, from history's beginnings to the present day. They have always excited man's interest and curiosity. From early times, dreams were felt to possess meaning and significance.

All of us differ in the number of dreams we can remember, even though new research has shown that we all dream during four or five dream periods a night.

Almost everyone, however, has awakened some mornings with the memory of a dream fresh and vivid in his mind. Most people are able to recall one or two childhood dreams that were experienced over and over. You can probably recall several dreams you have had during your life; and, if you are one of the lucky "dream recallers," you can remember one of the dreams you had last night. Most of us, too, have awakened in the middle of the night from the midst of a dream.

Although the experience of dreaming is common, it is hard to define a dream. Since dreaming occurs only during sleep, one can never actually say "I am dreaming." Thus our knowledge of dreams must always be "after-the-fact." That is, our knowledge of dreams is only memory of dreams. We are never able consciously and rationally to *observe* our dream as we dream it, though sometimes we have the vague sense that we are doing so. Some physiologists now want to define dreaming by a certain combination of EEG patterns and eye movements. Theirs is a good experimental working definition. Most of us, though, still hold to a notion of dreams as some mental, visual experience occurring during sleep that we identify as a dream after awakening from it. Webster's Dictionary defines dreaming as "A sequence of sensations, images, thoughts, etc., passing through a sleeping person's mind." Others prefer to regard dreams as sleeping hallucinations, because there is a similarity between the dreams of normal people and the hallucinations of mentally ill people or users of drugs.

By its very nature, then, the dream is a mysterious event. It seems to bridge reality and illusion, fact and fantasy. A Japanese writer, reflecting on this, observed: "Last night I dreamed I was a butterfly. Now I am not sure if I am a man who dreamed he was a butterfly, or a butterfly who now dreams he is a man."

Even though dreams are often composed of recognizable, ordinary people and daily objects, the logic of dreams is quite unlike that of our usual lives. Time seems unimportant: events whirl upon one another. Space is easily bridged: we are now in one spot; then, an instant later, in another. People who are dead or unrecognizable appear in dreams. Bizarre costumes are common; strange actions take place. Parts of one person or place are connected with parts of another person or place. Language seems strange; words take on new meaning. Sometimes we are terrified or angry in dreams; sometimes we see colors, feel pain, or even taste things. Anything that happens to us in real life can happen in a dream, but so can a fantastic number of unusual and unreal things.

It is no wonder then that, as far back as ancient Egypt, men have tried to unravel the mysteries of dreams. And most people have agreed that dreams have meaning. Some have even thought that dreams are divinely inspired and can foretell the future.

Some of the best-known ancient dreams are those concerning the biblical Joseph. He may be considered the first famous dream analyst. Joseph, the second youngest of Jacob's sons, was envied by his brothers for being Jacob's favorite. One night he dreamed as follows: "We were binding sheaves in the field, and lo, my sheaf arose, and also stood upright; and behold, your sheaves stood round about and made obeisance to my sheaf." The brothers thought this dream represented Joseph's desire to outdo them, and they feared that he would succeed. They tried to punish him. The dream, which was probably indicative of Joseph's personal feelings, did prove to foretell the future. Joseph became a great man in Egypt, assisting Pharaoh. His way to fame with Pharaoh, interestingly enough, was also through dreams. He interpreted two dreams of Pharaoh's that had confused the Egyptian dreamologists:

*Behold, Pharaoh stood by the river. And behold there came up out of the river seven well-favored kine and fatfleshed; and they fed in a meadow. And, behold, seven other kine came up after them out of the river, ill-favored and lean-fleshed; and stood by the other*

*kine on the brink of the river. And the ill-favored*
*and lean-fleshed kine did eat up the seven well-favored*
*and fat kine.*

Pharaoh's second dream repeated this occurrence, but
ears of corn replaced the cattle. Joseph interpreted
this as a prophecy of seven years of plenty followed
by seven harsh years. He suggested that Pharaoh fill
the granaries over the seven good years to prepare for

forthcoming famine. The interpretation turned out to be correct.

This biblical view of dreams and the use made of them coincides with early men's view of dreams as divinely inspired prophecies having little to do with the dreamer's own wishes. Primitive people today still share this view. Dreams are considered omens of future events. Another common primitive belief is that during sleep the soul migrates, leaving the body and actually experiencing what is dreamed. Thus it is able to meet spirits, ghosts, and other souls or to travel to far-off places. The Kiwai Papuans of British New Guinea believe that if a sorcerer catches the soul of a dreamer on its travels the dreamer can be kept permanently asleep. A New Guinea native who awoke with aches and pains decided that during his dreams his soul had been beaten by another soul. One Pacific islander dreamed that his boss had made him work extra hard at his daytime job; when he awoke he spoke bitterly to the boss for extending his job into the nighttime. Children in Eastern Europe are warned to sleep with their mouths closed so that their souls cannot escape.

The wish to understand dreams has led to "dream books," handy guides to interpreting dream symbols according to current notions of the day. Dream books have been circulated since 1800 B.C. in Egypt and were common in 650 B.C. in Assyria. They were popular in ancient Greece and Rome, throughout the Middle

Ages, and even have a certain popularity in our own age. Today, most drugstore paperback book counters have at least one pamphlet on dream interpretation.

The ancient Greeks had several views on dreams. The philosopher Socrates apparently felt that dreams represent the voice of conscience. His student Plato believed that dreams express the irrational in all of us: "Even in good men, there is a lawless wild-beast nature, which peers out in sleep." Aristotle believed that some dreams could be rational and some accidental. His objection to taking all dreams seriously was perhaps related to his rebellion against the irrational religious cults that had sprung up in his day.

The Romans kept up the interest in dreams as a prediction of future events. Lucretius, however, added the insight that a night's dreams deal with the very things that interest us in the daytime or with bodily needs that dreaming satisfies.

Little new was added to the understanding of dreams until the end of the nineteenth century. At that time, in an age of science, "learned" people considered dreams to be an effect of indigestion; dreams were felt to be meaningless by many "educated" people. If a door creaked, they reasoned, you dreamed of a burglar. If your forehead was wet, you dreamed of water or wine or swimming. Scientists avoided the subject of dreams until a Viennese doctor, Sigmund Freud, began to study them.

Freud laid the foundation of our modern knowledge of dreams. He was the first person to glimpse their relation to the unconscious. To understand Freud's insight, you must first understand how he became interested in dreams and then how dreams, because of Freud, became an object of research by psychiatrists and psychologists instead of by philosophers and poets.

Freud was a physician and a scientist. He shared the viewpoint of the nineteenth century scientists and philosophers that all natural processes follow an orderly determined pattern. He extended this notion to cover the causes of dreams.

Freud's interest in dreams came at the same time as his "self-analysis," the first psychoanalysis ever carried out. It began in 1897, shortly after the death of his father, a loss that triggered deep feelings in Freud. At the same time, he was learning to probe the dreams of his patients, and he began to wonder about their purpose and meaning. He studied them by a technique known as free association, asking his patients what ideas came to their minds as they discussed their dreams. The results of his studies were published in 1900 in his classic book *The Interpretation of Dreams.*

Dreams to Freud were an area of human experience that could not be explained by existing theories of psychology. Freud came to his understanding of the unconscious by working with hysterics, patients who suffered from paralysis or other spells with physical

symptoms but for which there was no apparent physical cause. Instead, the symptoms were caused by emotions that the patients were unaware they had. Freud
called these unconscious feelings "repressed emotions." He discovered that the dreams of such patients
often reveal the repressed feelings that caused the
trouble. They reveal wishes that the patient could
not accept consciously until they are brought out into
the open and discussed.

Freud believed that all of us carry around these
wishes and desires, which are removed from our conscious state. Usually we repress them, but at night
when we go to sleep these feelings are at last able to
come out in the form of dreams.

Some dreams, like children's dreams, are obvious
and straightforward. This class of dreams often repre-
sents clear fulfilment of a wish aroused the previous
day. For instance, a two-year-old child who had to give
a friend a basket of cherries he wanted for himself
related his dream, "Hermann eaten all the cherries."
A three-year-old girl who enjoyed her first boat trip
and did not want to end it dreamed that "I was sailing
on the lake." In childhood dreams, which are not
meaningless, Freud found a direct, undisguised state-
ment of a wish. He felt this "wish-fulfilment" is the
essence of dreams.

In the dreams of adults, though, the feelings do
not come out in a precise, clear way. Only by studying

and analyzing the dreams is it possible, Freud believed, to find out exactly what they mean. What a patient remembers of a dream Freud called "the manifest dream content." But the story of the dream often differs from its real meaning, "the latent dream content," and this meaning was the one brought out by analysis. Freud believed that each dreamer transforms his real feelings into acceptable form by means of a sort of mental "censor." Events of the previous day would be used by the "censor" and incorporated into the dream to mask its real meaning. This masking serves the purpose of protecting the dreamer's sleep, for, according to Freud, if the dream revealed the true meaning, it could be so horrifying that it would awaken the sleeper.

Recently, the "dream censor" theory has been brought into question. Many scientists today view dreams as simply random events in our nervous system, triggered at intervals during the night by a "dream center." The dream images and their associations would be the ones we were most concerned with at the time. The dream, of course, is still meaningful, for studying its images leads us to the unconscious feelings and conflicts we are most concerned with. Most psychiatrists still think that the things we put in our dreams reflect our most crucial feelings and wishes.

Thus dreams appear to be almost like a detective

story, with false clues, concealments, and so on. In addition, dream symbols are used as substitutes for objects and people. For example, a red dress may represent a girl who is remembered wearing it. Time and space may be warped to condense and disguise the latent dream. And all of this, according to Freud, may be for the purpose of preventing us from being awakened or from recognizing the true meaning of the frightening images we have repressed from our awareness.

Of course, not all dreams conceal anxiety and terror. Some transform longings for love, desire for power, or strivings for advancement. Often, however, the dream is constructed in such a way that repressed feelings are hidden. The following case is an example:

*A young man dreamed that his mother's face was severely burned by a hot frying pan. He awoke feeling upset and sorrowful, wondering how he could have dreamed such a horrible thing. Analysis revealed that he had been angry at his mother the previous day and had had the thought, "I wish she were dead and would leave me alone." This thought was repugnant to him, and he repressed it. The anger was also repressed. It emerged at night, and the mother was injured. In the dream, however, the young man escaped blame, for it was not his "fault."*

Since much of repressed material is either sexual or aggressive, dreams naturally deal with these themes. More than one hundred common symbols for the male and female genitals have been listed; they are usually based on a similarity in shape or function. Aggressive acts are frequently carried out, as in the example above, without the dreamer's "really" being guilty. Yet whose dream is it, after all, and where does the thought come from?

Freud listed these as some common types of dreams:

1. Dreams of being naked, he felt, concealed the wish for recapturing the early childhood paradise of unashamed nakedness.

2. Dreams of falling were felt to represent the danger of surrender to sexual temptation.

3. Dreams of water and swimming were seen as often dealing with birth.

4. Dreams of being paralyzed dealt with inhibitions of either sexual or aggressive impulses.

5. Dreams of robbers or burglars often represented the father, seen as a threatening, punishing figure.

Freud refrained, as do contemporary psychiatrists, from using dream books or assuming that dream symbols are interchangeable from person to person. The meaning of a dream element to each individual dreamer is what is important. Thus a snake may represent a male sexual object to one person, a circus to another, and a dangerous camping trip to a third. A

hat may be a sexual symbol or it may stand for one's
father who wore a hat or it may represent status or
occupation.

The most prominent addition to Freud's understanding of dreams came from one of his students, the
Swiss psychiatrist Carl Jung. For a period the two men
worked closely, but then, in 1913, after a dispute over
the relative importance of sexual elements in the unconscious, they split. Jung believed that in addition to
the personal unconscious, which contained both sexual

and aggressive feelings, and from which dreams emerged, there was a "collective" unconscious, a part of our mind that carries with it memories of earlier, more primitive epochs in human development. He felt that all men share this element of the unconscious, that its images, projected in dreams, speak for vast centuries of common human experience. Jung interpreted some dreams as going beyond the dreamer's own experience and conflicts to represent collective symbols that have meaning for all people. These symbols are also found in myth and other forms of art. Often, Jung felt, such dreams have religious meaning.

For example, a woman who dreams of going to a religious shrine, painstakingly making her way to the altar, being forced to bow every few steps, but finally reaching her goal, brings to Jung's mind the essence of religious experience and searching for truth that is common to all men.

Jung himself felt, of course, that many dreams have almost entirely personal meaning. Only some dreams deal with collective material. For example, an acquaintance confided to him the following dream:

*I am climbing a high mountain over steep, snow-covered slopes. I mount higher and higher—it is marvelous weather. The higher I climb, the better I feel. I think, "If only I could go on climbing like this forever!" When I reach the top, my happiness and elation are so strong that I feel I could mount right up into space. And I discover that I actually can do this. I go on climbing on empty air. I awake in a real ecstasy.*

Jung told his friend, "My dear man, I know you can't give up mountain climbing, but let me implore you not to go alone from now on. When you go, take two guides, and you must promise on your word of honor to follow their directions." The man laughed. Two months later, he was buried by an avalanche but lived; three months after that he was killed. A friend observing him reported that he literally stepped out into the air as he was descending a rock wall. He was dashed to pieces far below. Jung had grasped the personal message in the dream and tried to alert the man to it.

Jung's emphasis in later years on the collective unconscious and common symbols in art and dreams made him a favorite with artists and poets. Most psychoanalysts, while admiring his innovation and his learning, have been unable to accept his idea of a predetermined collective memory. Most agree, though, that he added new dimensions to our understanding of dreams, especially in linking them to primitive religion, myth, poetry, art, and the early concepts of dreams as divinely sent prophecies or inspiration.

Does anyone know what "normal" dreams are like?

Until a hundred years ago, there were many ideas about what dreams mean, but no one had collected large numbers of dreams to see what they are really about. In the past century, however, dream researchers have begun making vast tabulations of dream data. Clear patterns have emerged, enabling them to put "normal" dreams into definite categories.

We know now, for instance, that most of our dreams occur in familiar settings. One third of all dreams take place in a house; one quarter occur on trains, buses, airplanes, boats, subways, or roads; one tenth, in party or social gathering settings; another tenth, out of doors, as on farms.

Almost every dream includes the dreamer, sometimes as a mere spectator, at other times as a participant. This is thought to reflect how active or passive the dreamer tends to be in real life. Other dream figures are family members and friends. Even so, about 40 percent of the people who appear in dreams cannot be identified. These may be thought of, in Jung's terms, as symbolic characters. From a view closer to Freud's, they may be felt to be significant family or friends who are not identified because of repression. That is, if you dream of being pursued by a strange man with a club, he may in fact represent your father, but you will be unable to identify him as your father because realizing who he is would be threatening and upsetting. Much of the work of psychotherapy consists of bringing such unconscious feeling to the patient's awareness and talking away the guilt and fear that accompany it by making the patient understand the reasons for such feeling.

The action in dreams is much like our childhood action. Walking, dancing, playing ball, running, and such activities are found in about one third of all dreams. Observing others or simply talking is found in one quarter of all dreams. Also found, of course, are echoes of our daily activities, such as studying and working. Sexual activity is very common in dreams. Violence is less common but not infrequent.

Many dreams deal with sad, angry, or frightened feelings. More sophisticated feelings, such as envy, pride, peevishness, and curiosity, are found less frequently than are our basic emotions.

Most psychiatrists are interested more in what the dreams mean to the dreamer in his own life situation than in a description of the events alone. Everyone can make associations about one person's dream, and often very interesting analyses may be given. But only the dreamer's associations tell what *his* dream "really" means.

If we all dream during four or five periods a night, why can we not remember more dreams than we do? This question has recently found some answers. Although we do dream many times a night, there are two factors that influence our remembering. The first is physical; if we are awakened by accident—a buzzer, a fire-engine outside, an alarm clock—in the midst of a dream, we can usually recall it with much detail. We usually recall color, the exact situations of the dream, our feelings, and so on. If we are awakened after a dream period is finished, our recall is much less; we may recall an image or a fragment of a dream. Also, color seems to fade from our memory: the recall we have tends to be in black and white. Awakening in the morning, we may remember only a few fragments of our entire night's dreaming or nothing at all. In addition, a psychological factor may influence dream recall. If, as is generally believed, dreams deal with our inner unconscious feelings and fantasies, we will tend to repress the memory of these dreams. The dream material may be too distressing, too frightening, too anxiety-provoking to recall. We can recall manifest dream material more readily if the latent content is well disguised. More easily interpreted dreams tend to be forgotten. Even nightmares, which awaken us from sleep with their horrifying imagery, are usually forgotten by the time we wake up in the morning after having fallen back to sleep. You may have had the experience of jotting down some phrases about a dream in the middle of the night and finding them vague and incomprehensible in the morning. Our minds have drawn a veil over this memory. Forgetting our dreams is apparently linked both to physi-

ological processes and to emotional factors that tend to keep much dream material from our conscious minds.

Many people today still conceive of dreams as haphazard, meaningless, and accidental; still others, believing that dreams are significant, consult dream books or tell one another their dreams, hoping to make some sense of them. Beyond the notion of wishfulfilment and sexual symbols, though, most people are uninformed about the interpretation of dreams. Dream interpretation has been refined into an art, however, in the practice of psychoanalysis and psychotherapy. Here, dreams are used as a "window" to see into the unconscious of the patient. A patient's main internal conflicts, as well as his repressed impulses and fears, appear in his dream production. When a patient can recall a dream, the analyst makes use of it. The technique of dream interpretation is simple and can actually be practiced by any intelligent person. The guiding (and most difficult!) principle is complete honesty.

Early in psychoanalysis, Freud learned that the spontaneous "free associations" the patient produces reveal unconscious processes by following trains of association that the patient is unaware of. The dream is explored by the same process. First, the patient relates the manifest dream. The psychiatrist is interested in clarifying the action of the dream, the dreamer's feelings, the dreamer's role in the dream, the perception of other people or things. Then, with the manifest dream in hand, the psychiatrist begins to interpret—that is, to unravel the symbolic language of the dream and get at the latent material.

Dream research goes on at a dizzying pace. Dreaming, too, goes on at the same prolific, fascinating pace—four or five periods of dreaming a night per person—it has for centuries. As we understand more about the physiology of the dream process, we come closer to probing the function dreams provide for our body. Since Freud's pioneering work in 1900, we have also come to understand more about what dreams say to us about ourselves and our inner feelings. The use of dreams in psychotherapy will probably not diminish. Interest in our own dreams, as a way of understanding our inner selves and of appreciating the depth of the creative process within each of us, will continue. In addition, the experience each of us has, from time to time, as we awake from sleep, the bizarre, colorful, puzzling content of a dream still fresh in our minds, will continue to tantalize and excite us and to urge us further in our search to fulfill one of the oldest injunctions of mankind: "Know thyself." The untamed frontier within ourselves remains.

# III

## A Different Kind of Sleep

In April, 1952, a young graduate student at the University of Chicago unknowingly made the biggest contribution to understanding dreams since Freud. The student, Eugene Aserinsky, who was working in the laboratory of Nathaniel Kleitman, one of the original sleep researchers, was watching the pattern of a sleeping infant's brain waves on an electroencephalograph. Suddenly he noticed that one of the recording pens was jumping wildly up and down, and his immediate reaction was that the machine must be broken. But when he went to check, he found nothing wrong with the machine. Instead it was the baby's eyes that were causing the movements of the pen. Under his closed lids the subject's eyes were rapidly rolling around.

Aserinsky reported his finding to Kleitman, and for the next several months the two worked to find out what it might mean. They tried waking up adult subjects during the periods when their eyes were moving, and one thing immediately became clear. Almost all of them were dreaming or at least reported that they had clear detailed memories of a dream. Yet, if the scientists awakened the subjects when their eyes were not moving, almost none of them could remember dreaming, and the ones who could had only vague memories.

For the first time in history it was clear that there really was a physical difference between dreaming sleep and nondreaming sleep. In September, five months after Aserinsky's discovery, he and Kleitman published a paper on the subject of REM's, as they had come to call the rapid eye movements that accompanied dreaming sleep. But like many totally new discoveries, this one did not seem to make any great impression on the scientific world. Among the first people to exhibit any interest in it was a group of New York researchers at Downstate Medical Center in Brooklyn. They had visited Kleitman's laboratory and, being a little skeptical of his findings, wanted to check them. The experimenters used one group of subjects who reported dreaming often and another group who claimed not to dream at all. They tried waking both groups during REM and non-REM periods of sleep. What they found dramatically confirmed Kleitman and Aserinsky's findings. Even the nondreamers reported that they were dreaming almost half of the times they were awakened in REM sleep. The frequent-dreamers reported dreams after 93 percent of such awakenings. As Kleitman later pointed out, the evidence is overwhelming that everyone dreams, but some people are better at remembering than others. Dreamers and nondreamers, he said, should be reclassified as recallers and nonrecallers.

Eventually, more researchers became attracted to the new field of sleep research, and for several years the leading investigator was an energetic medical student, William Dement, who took Aserinsky's place in Kleitman's laboratory. Dement started his investigations by making EEG records of sleeping subjects' brain waves, a technique that had already provided much of what was known about sleep. But instead of merely taking sample recordings at intervals during the night, he left the machine turned on all night long. The method soon paid off in a number of significant findings.

One of the first things Dement discovered was that

periods of REM sleep, which seemed to correspond exactly to periods of dreaming, were not random events caused by some noise or other occurrence in the outside world, as some people had assumed. Instead, the dream periods appeared with great regularity at approximately ninety-minute intervals throughout the night. The REM periods always occurred in Stage 1 of sleep. Except for a brief period at the beginning of the night, this stage (when the brain waves are the closest to those of the waking state) was always accompanied by REM's and by dreaming.

Dement soon found himself staying awake two or three nights a week in order to find out more about the pattern of dreaming sleep. He discovered that all his subjects experienced from four to seven REM periods a night, each lasting about twenty minutes but becoming increasingly long as the night wore on. By waking up his subjects during the REM periods, he found that each period included several different dreams, which were usually separated by some movements of the body and a brief awakening.

Dement's findings had contradicted several popular notions about the process of dreaming. They disproved the idea many people still have that dreams only seem to occur over a period of time but actually happen in a flash. He found that the time that the dream seems to take, according to the dreamer, is about the same as the actual time that he spends dreaming. Freud's theory that dreams are "the guardian of sleep" also suffered from Dement's findings. Not only did his subjects wake up in between their dreams, but it turned out that dreams did not serve the purpose of explaining away noises or other stimuli that happen during the night. Dement found that it was impossible to bring on a dream no matter what he did to the subject, unless the person was already in a period of REM sleep. On the other hand, he could modify a dream that was already in progress. For instance, if he spilled water on a subject, the dream might switch to one about a waterfall. But the subject was not made to dream because of the stimulus. He would have dreamed anyway.

In an effort to find out more about what kind of outside stimuli could influence the content of dreams, Dement and another Chicago researcher, Edward A. Wolpert, disproved the popular idea that hunger and thirst are a cause of dreams. They asked three volunteers to go without fluid for twenty-four hours before coming to the sleep laboratory and then report the stories of each of their dreams. Although all the subjects were very thirsty when they went to sleep, not one of them had a dream about drinking or even about being thirsty.

However, Ralph Berger, a researcher working in Edinburgh, Scotland, found a different kind of stimulus that did affect the content of a subject's dreams.

In one of his experiments he tried saying aloud the names of girl friends and boy friends of a group of Edinburgh students while the young people were sleeping in his laboratory. Frequently the subjects incorporated the sounds of the names into their dreams, even though they did not actually dream about their friends. For instance when Berger mentioned the name Jenny to one young man, the student dreamed of opening a safe with a "jemmy." Mentioning Sheila to another student made him dream about a book he was reading by Schiller. Interestingly enough, the students reacted best to the names of their own friends; they rarely reacted to the name of someone else's friend.

All over the world people were learning more and more about the process of dreaming. Yet no one knew what made people dream. And no one knew how dreams were related to REM's. At first many researchers thought that the eye movements probably were caused by the fact that sleepers actually "watched" their dreams; that their eyes followed the action of the dreams. Dement collected some of the first evidence for this theory when he noticed that one of his sleep subjects was having eye movements that were all straight up and down, with none from side to side. He then decided that if this ever happened again, he would wake up the sleeper and ask him what he was dreaming about. Soon he had collected several of these people, and the eye movements were so closely related to the subjects of their dreams that it did seem as if they had been watching the events as they happened. One had dreamed of climbing a series of ladders, another of watching climbers on a cliff, another of shooting baskets, and another of watching leaflets floating down from a blimp.

He found one person whose eyes moved consistently from side to side with no up and down movements. This person reported that he had been dreaming of two people throwing tomatoes at each other.

Another critical piece of evidence for the theory came from a study of blind people. People who have been blind since birth or for most of their lives dream, but they do not see things in their dreams. Ian Oswald, working in Edinburgh, Scotland, wondered whether such people had REM's or not. If they did, it would indicate that REM's were not simply the result of a sleeper watching his dreams, for in these people there was nothing to watch. Oswald had some difficulty in persuading people to come and sleep in the mental hospital where he was conducting his experiments, but eventually he found two men who had been blind since childhood and did not picture things in their dreams. Neither of them had REM's. Yet three blind subjects who had been blind for only a short time did see things in their dreams and did have rapid eye movements.

Still another piece of evidence for the look-at-dreams theory came from cats. A study of the brainwaves in the part of the brain which organizes vision showed that the nerve cells there were very active during REM periods just as they were when the cats were awake and looking around. Yet they were inactive when cats were awake but had their eyes closed, and they were inactive during regular sleep. Thus it appeared that the cats watched their dreams in much the same way that they watched things when they were awake.

Yet it is not possible to fully accept this theory even

now, for there is some conflicting evidence. New-born babies, for instance, who do not yet have the ability to see images, have very active REM's. As yet nobody really knows exactly what REM's mean.

Gradually the subject of REM's became so complicated that investigators began seeking new methods to study it. Again Dement was a leader in the field. He credits his wife with suggesting a method, which was to determine the purpose of REM sleep by finding out what happens to a person who is deprived of it.

The process of depriving people of REM sleep and observing what effect it had on them turned out to be more complicated than anyone expected. A typical subject had to spend several nights in the sleep laboratory so that his normal sleep pattern could be recorded with the EEG. Then, for up to a week, Dement or one of his colleagues would allow the subject to sleep but would awaken him every time he slipped into REM sleep. He then would be allowed to sleep normally for several days while being studied to see what effect the deprivation period had had on his normal sleep patttern.

One effect of depriving people of REM sleep became clear immediately. When a subject was deprived, he did his best to make up for the lost REM sleep even though he was getting a normal amount of regular, or non-REM, sleep. During the first night of the deprivation period he might have to be awakened four or five times to keep him from getting REM sleep, but as the deprivation period continued, the number of awakenings had to be increased. By the fourth or fifth night, it would be necessary to wake him up about twenty times, as he tried more and more often to get some REM sleep. The first night after the deprivation period was over and the subject was allowed as much REM sleep as he wanted, he might spend 40 percent of his time in that phase as opposed to the normal 20 percent.

Presumably if this stage of sleep was so important that people tried their best to make it up when they went without it, REM sleep must have some very important function in the body. Dement studied his subjects carefully to see what might be missing after they were deprived of REM sleep. But to his surprise, he did not find anything very significant. Some of the people seemed to be a little more anxious and irritable, some had difficulty concentrating, and some, including Dement (who was his own fourth subject), seemed abnormally hungry. Although these results were not too conclusive, Dement put forth the theory that depriving a subject of REM sleep, which meant depriving him of dreaming, increased his basic instinctive drives, such as the drive to eat. Perhaps dreams operated as a safety valve, to let out excessive instinctive desires in a harmless way. If a person was deprived of his dreams, these drives would be present to an abnormal degree in the daytime.

However, Dement was not really satisfied with these results, and he wondered what would happen if he deprived a subject of dreams for a period much longer than one week. Perhaps in his earlier experiments he had not been depriving the subjects of enough dreams to show up a real abnormality.

Finally he found a volunteer to undergo what turned out to be a very strenuous test. A young artist agreed to undergo deprivation of REM sleep until what Dement called "dramatic changes" occurred. Each night the artist would come to the sleep lab, where he would be awakened every time the EEG showed signs that he was slipping into REM sleep. But to be even more certain that the deprivation was total, Dement gave him a watchman's clock, which had to be punched every fifteen minutes throughout the day to make sure that the artist did not take any unscheduled naps. Everything went well for four or five nights; as expected, the artist needed more and more awakenings to prevent his getting REM sleep. But then the number of awakenings began to level off, and Dement suspected that the artist was getting some sleep during the day. Perhaps he was using an alarm clock to rouse him in time to punch the watchman's clock.

There seemed only one solution to the problem—

to have someone follow the subject wherever he went and make sure that he did not get any sleep.

With this check, the artist's attempts to dream became more and more frequent. He would have to be awakened more than thirty times, and even shouting "fire" in his ear failed to wake him. After thirteen nights Dement had to give up the experiment, because the only way to keep the artist from dreaming was to haul him out of bed and drag him around to keep him awake. In other words, he had to be deprived of *all* sleep, because whenever he went to sleep he would immediately start having rapid eye movements.

To Dement the experiment was disappointing. The artist had been under tremendous pressure to dream, and yet nothing significant had happened to his personality other than that he became somewhat irritable. And this finding could have been a result of his not getting much sleep of any kind.

While Dement was studying REM sleep in people, other researchers had discovered that it also exists in other animals. Their studies were beginning to show that there is more to the state of REM sleep than just dreaming. Although most of them had started out to study dreams, they found that the state of dreaming sleep is even more important.

The pioneer investigator of REM sleep in animals was a French researcher named Michel Jouvet who had done a great deal of work on the subject and had come up with some amazing findings. First he made a careful record of the behavior of sleeping cats, which has been invaluable to other researchers ever since. As he described the process, a cat curls up into a tight ball with its neck bent when it first goes to sleep. At this point it is in light sleep and can be easily awakened. As it passes into deep sleep, its muscles go completely slack, and at the same time it starts having REM's. It may breathe rapidly for a moment and its legs and whiskers may twitch. (All these actions are easy to observe on a pet cat at home.) Because the eyes and brain of a cat are very active during REM sleep, while its muscles are limp, Jouvet called the stage paradoxical sleep. But we shall call it REM sleep, as it is called in humans.

One of Jouvet's most important contributions was

separating REM sleep from dreaming. He performed brain operations on a group of cats which deprived them of the part of the brain responsible for thinking, seeing, and hearing—all the activities necessary for dreaming. Therefore one could say that his cats did not dream. Yet when he recorded them with the EEG, he found that they still had eye movements and that these alternated with a state resembling wakefulness. Obviously the REM's in these cats were not caused by their dreams, because they had no dreams.

With such experiments in mind, Dement too decided to switch to cats for his experiments on REM deprivation. After finding a small room and an office at Stanford Medical Center in California, he proceeded to get his first two cats. The first he named Gray Fang (because it had bitten one of his assistants), and the second he named Yellow Fang. In order to make it easier to take brain-wave recordings from the sleeping animals, he implanted wires directly into their brains. These wires terminated in an electrical outlet, set into their skulls. Whenever he wanted to take a recording, he merely plugged wires from the EEG into the outlets on their skulls. Although the procedure sounds horrifying, the animals were anesthetized for the operation and after they recovered seemed to be in no discomfort at all.

Dement decided to deprive Gray Fang of REM sleep while depriving Yellow Fang of regular sleep. This way he could be sure that any effects Gray Fang showed would be due to his loss of REM sleep in particular and not merely to a loss of sleep in general. Both cats would spend eight hours of their day having brain-waves recorded while they slept and the rest of the time they would stay awake.

One of Dement's main reasons for switching from people to cats was to test an idea he had that REM sleep was caused by a chemical piling up in the brain. He thought that during wakefulness the chemical might increase and when it reached a certain amount it might trigger REM sleep. The REM sleep would get rid of the chemical and then the process would start over again. To check this idea he decided to take some fluid from Gray Fang's brain after the cat had been deprived of REM sleep for a while. Presumably the deprivation should cause the chemical to pile up in his brain. Then he would inject this fluid into Yellow Fang who had had plenty of REM sleep. If Yellow Fang fell into REM sleep, it would indicate that Gray Fang's fluid did, indeed, contain an REM-inducing chemical.

After a month, the results of the study were again not very conclusive. Gray Fang did not seem to be acting abnormally, although Dement was not sure that he was being deprived of all his REM sleep. The process of transferring fluid from Gray Fang to Yellow Fang turned out to be very difficult. In one successful transfer, however, Gray Fang's fluid did seem to make Yellow Fang get slightly more REM sleep, but one success was not enough.

On the basis of these preliminary tests, Dement decided that the principle of the experiments was worthwhile, and he resolved to continue them with a larger number of cats. His assistant, Peter Henry, worked out a new way to keep the cats awake while they were not being monitered on the EEG. With a couple of rolling pins and a washing machine motor, he rigged up a treadmill so that they would have to keep walking slowly and would not get a chance to fall asleep until it was time for them to be studied.

This second study went on twenty-four hours a day for two and a half months. At the end there were a few more interesting results. One cat, Othello, had been deprived of REM sleep for seventy days, and some of the others for nearly as long. As Dement and his colleagues had reluctantly come to expect, there were no drastic changes in the cats' behavior. But there was one measurable change. The brains of the cats deprived of REM sleep were in a much more excited state than normal and reacted much more rapidly to noise.

Dement was more puzzled than ever. How could REM sleep be so desperately important that the animals did anything they could to make it up (one cat learned to dash to the end of the treadmill and catch a few winks on the ride back) and yet cause no significant ill-effects when they went without it for long periods of time. "What can it be for?" Dement asked over and over again, "Is it some sort of cosmic joke?"

The discovery of the increased excitability of the cats' brains made Dement wonder about some of the minor changes he had seen in the cats' behavior. One animal, a black male named Proteus, seemed to have an increased mating drive after a long period without REM sleep. Other cats showed increased appetites and restlessness. This reminded Dement of some of the symptoms exhibited by the first people deprived of REM sleep. Perhaps they, too, were related to the brain's increased excitability.

He wondered if maybe the lack of REM sleep caused a chemical to pile up in the part of the brain that controls the basic drives of hunger and mating. An animal that had been deprived of REM sleep would have an excess of the chemical and therefore would exhibit stronger drives.

After thinking about these problems, Dement decided to do another experiment with cats and to look more carefully for signs of increased basic drives. Jouvet had devised a way of preventing cats from getting REM sleep by putting them on a brick in a cage filled with a few inches of water. The cat could sleep in its normal, slightly crouched position, but whenever it started to fall into REM sleep, its neck would go limp, its head would hit the water, and this would wake it up. Dement decided to try Jouvet's method.

The plan of his third experiment called for each cat to spend twenty hours a day sitting on its brick and then spend three hours off the brick having EEG recordings taken. During the three hours, each time a cat went into REM sleep, it was awakened. The remaining hour was spent getting exercise.

The results of these new experiments seemed to confirm the belief that the cats showed greater basic drives after being deprived of REM sleep. Proteus, who had shown an increased mating drive during the earlier experiments, would try to mate with any cat brought near him after he had been deprived of REM sleep. But when he was allowed to make up the lost sleep, this abnormal behavior disappeared entirely. Othello

did not experience any change in mating drive, but he did prowl around incessantly looking for food. He, too, got over this behavior when he was allowed to make up his lost REM sleep.

Even after all these experiments, the nature and causes of REM sleep remain a mystery. As we shall see in the next chapter, more and more evidence is accumulating that, at least in animals, a brain chemical is responsible for bringing on this stage. But why do we need REM sleep, and why do we dream? Nobody knows. Yet there must be a very important reason for it, since every mammal that has been studied so far has turned out to have REM's. It is hard to imagine that this happens for no reason.

One possible explanation is that REM sleep is a process important in the development of the brain before birth and perhaps for a while after it. Evidence from babies and young animals would seem to confirm this idea. New-born babies spend about half their sleeping time in the REM phase, and new-born kittens, which are born in a very immature stage, spend their entire sleep in REM's. Perhaps REM sleep in adults is merely a hangover of a process that has a function only in the developing brain.

But if this is the case, why do adult animals and people try so hard to make up for lost REM sleep? If a person is deprived long enough, he will fall into REM sleep so often that he gets no non-REM sleep at all. It would seem as if REM sleep is even more important than regular sleep.

All we really can say now is that Aserinsky, Kleitman, Dement, Jouvet, and all the scientists who have worked with them have discovered a third state of existence. Before their work, we knew only about sleep and wakefulness. But now we know that there is a different kind of sleep—the mysterious state of REM sleep and dreaming.

## IV
# Why Do We Sleep?

Have you ever wondered why you go to sleep each night? Why do you sleep only once every twenty-four hours instead of seven or eight times the way a new-born baby does? Why do you get only six to ten hours of sleep a day when a cat gets about seventeen? If you think about it, you will probably reply, "I sleep because I get tired, and sleep refreshes a tired body." Your explanation is certainly correct, and most scientists would agree with it. Yet it does not seem to be the complete answer. If the purpose of sleep is only to refresh a tired body, why does a baseball player, exhausted after a hard game, wait until his regular bedtime to go to sleep? Why does he not drop off as soon as he reaches the locker room? Why does a businessman who spends his eight-hour working day sitting in a comfortable chair need just as much sleep as a farmer who exercises vigorously for twelve or fourteen hours a day?

Questions like these have puzzled mankind for centuries. Even primitive men had an explanation. They thought that sleep was necessary because it freed the soul to enter the world of spirits. They believed that people's souls are imprisoned in their bodies during the day but that at night they can get out and wander.

By the sixth century B.C. people were seeking more scientific explanations. The first theory on record was set down by a Greek physician named Alcmeon, who thought that sleep was caused by the motion of blood in the veins. A person gets sleepy, he said, when his blood flows out of his organs and settles in pools in his veins. He wakes up again when the blood flows back into his organs. A more plausible theory was proposed by the Greek philosopher and scientist Aristotle, who lived in the fourth century B.C. and was one of the most learned men of his day. He had noticed that people often fall asleep after eating a heavy meal. In the manner of all good scientists, he made up a theory that seemed to fit all the facts. If eating makes a person sleepy, he reasoned, then sleep must be caused by the process of digestion. At that time scientists believed that food gives off heat when it is digested. Heat, as Aristotle pointed out, always rises. In a person, the heat would rise from the stomach into the head and cause him to fall asleep. To clinch his argument, Aristotle pointed to one final piece of evidence. Everyone knows that new-born babies sleep most of the time. The reason, he stated, is that they eat so often. His theory also explained why babies have such large heads in proportion to the rest of their bodies. Since they eat frequently, heat constantly rises from their stomachs, and this heat eventually swells their heads.

Over the years scientists have proved that these explanations are incorrect, no matter how logical they may seem. It was not until relatively modern times, when medical researchers performed thousands of detailed experiments on sleeping animals and people, that anyone began to get a clear idea of what makes us sleep.

Today sleep is a major area of scientific research. All over the world doctors and scientists are working to find out what causes it. In 1965 the National Institute of Mental Health, a part of the United States Public Health Service that supports all types of research on the brain and mind, gave two million dollars in grants to researchers working on the mystery of sleep. These scientists pursue the subject from many different points of view. Some are psychiatrists, some are chemists, and others are brain specialists. All hope that they will eventually discover some clue, no matter how small, that will help to solve the big mystery of sleep. Most of them expect to find an explanation for sleep in one or both of the body's major control centers: the brain and the system of glands that regulate the body chemistry.

The body's master control center, the brain, is awesomely complex. It has been estimated that if an engineer wanted to build a working model of the brain he would need 1,300 rooms in which to set up his equipment, with a thousand billion, billion vacuum tubes and an equal number of wires. To run this gigantic machine he would need a million kilowatts of electric power. Yet the human brain, complex as it is, actually weighs only about three pounds and uses only about one fortieth of a kilowatt of power.

If you looked at a brain that had been removed from the skull, you would probably not be impressed with its appearance. It is about the color and consistency of tapioca and about the size of a grapefruit. Yet it controls almost everything that goes on in the body. Without a brain you could not think or see or feel or taste or move a muscle. The brain keeps your heart beating at the right rate, regulates your breathing, maintains your temperature at a more or less steady 98.6 degrees

Fahrenheit, and performs countless thousands of other tasks you are never even aware of.

To accomplish its enormous job, the brain acts somewhat like a telephone switchboard. Electrically coded messages enter it constantly from the body's sense organs: the eyes, ears, nose, tongue, and the organs in the skin that sense heat and cold, pressure and pain. The messages the sense organs send out travel to the brain along nerves, which are the body's equivalent of telephone wires. When the messages get to the brain, they are sorted out and classified. On the basis of the information it receives, the brain decides what action the body should take and sends messages out to specific muscles and organs, telling them what to do.

Let's illustrate how this process works; consider what happens when you accidentally cut your finger on a knife. Before you are even aware of the pain, a message rushes from your finger along a nerve into your spinal cord. This cord is a long column of nerve cells that runs up your backbone and connects your brain to the nerves in your body. Instantly another message races down to the muscles of your hand and arm telling them to jerk your finger away from the knife. While this is happening, a message travels toward a part of the brain called the thalamus. Suddenly you are aware of the pain, but you do not yet know what caused it or how bad it is. This awareness comes

when a message gets to the very top of your brain, a part called the cerebral cortex. The cortex sends out a variety of messages. One travels to the muscles of your face and mouth, causing you to grimace and to say "ouch." Another travels to your hand telling you to pick up the knife, so that you can see if there is blood on it. At the same time another part of your brain stores the information that knives are dangerous. You will be more careful next time.

You may wonder how the brain keeps all these messages straight. How does it tell the difference between a knife cut and a pin prick? Why does it never make a mistake and send a message to your foot when it should send one to your hand?

The reason for the brain's remarkable efficiency lies in the way it is constructed. The brain is certainly the most highly organized structure in the body. All its separate wrinkles and bulges have their own particular job, and they do not confuse themselves by trying to do the job of any other part. If you examined a brain you could see some of its major parts right away. The most conspicuous are two large wrinkled pouches called the cerebral hemispheres. The outer layer, or cortex, of these pouches is the thinking part of the brain. Here decisions are made and commands are given to the body. For some reason, the cortex of the left hemisphere controls the right side of the body, while the right hemisphere controls the left side. Both hemispheres are organized into separate parts, each of which controls a different area of the body. The parts that control the hands, the feet, and the tongue, for instance, are all separate so that their orders do not get mixed up.

The cerebral cortex is also the part of the brain that sorts out information coming in from the sense organs. If you are looking at a rose garden, for example, the cortex sorts out the messages coming in from your eyes and nose, so that you know the flowers are roses and not grass or weeds or chrysanthemums.

Just beneath the cerebral hemispheres lies a part of the brain called the cerebellum. This small lump of tissue has the enormous task of coordinating all the body's muscles. When the cerebrum gives the order to write, for instance, the cerebellum regulates the action of necessary muscles so that the proper motions are made. To get an idea of how complicated the cerebellum's task is, consider what it must do if it happens to be located in the brain of a concert pianist. This skilled performer can play from twenty to twenty-five notes a second, which requires that the muscles of his hands alone make four hundred or five hundred separate motions.

Although it would seem that the functions of the cerebral cortex and the cerebellum are absolutely necessary for survival, this is actually not the case. It is possible for a person to be kept alive without these parts of the brain. The brain centers necessary for life are far less conspicuous. Some of them lie at the very top of the spinal cord, in a region called the brainstem. This three-inch stalk contains centers that regulate such vital functions as the heartbeat, the flow of blood in the body, and breathing. In addition, there are centers there that control swallowing, coughing, and winking. A working brainstem is so necessary that a person can be killed merely by being hit hard on the part of the skull that lies over it.

Another vital center is a small lobe of tissue called

the hypothalamus, which is located above the roof of the mouth. This tiny pouch has turned out to have some remarkable powers and, as we shall see, also turns out to play an important role in sleep.

The functions of the hypothalamus were discovered first in animals. During the 1920's, a Swiss scientist, Walter R. Hess, became the first man to make it yield its secrets. To study the hypothalamus, he developed a technique that is now used to explore all areas of the brain and is proving to be extremely useful in sleep research. Hess decided that, since the brain sends and receives its messages by electricity, he might be able to find out what any part of the brain does by giving it a very small shock. The shock could be caused either by electricity or by injecting a chemical into the brain. Presumably this shock would cause the brain to send out a message identical to the one it normally sends when it receives a signal. To make sure that he delivered a shock only to the particular region of the brain that he was trying to study, Hess drilled a hole in the skull of an anesthetized animal and then pushed a very tiny insulated wire, called an electrode, directly into the brain. Only the tip of the wire was not insulated, and it was this part that delivered the shock. Today Hess's technique has been improved to the point where scientists can implant wires into a single brain cell, doing virtually no damage to surrounding cells. To make their work easier, they fasten an elec-

trical outlet to an animal's skull, leaving the wire electrodes permanently in the brain. To stimulate the
brain, they plug wires into the outlet and deliver a
shock. Hess's work has proved such a help to brain researchers that he was awarded a Nobel Prize in 1949.

In his early experiments Hess discovered that if he
implanted electrodes in a certain part of the hypothalamus and then sent in a tiny shock, the animal's
heart would slow down drastically. With the electrode
placed in another region, the shock would make the
heart speed up. Stimulating still other regions would
change the animal's blood pressure. Other researchers were quick to adopt the technique, and they found
even more surprising results. Stimulating one area of
the hypothalamus would cause an animal to eat and
eat, no matter how much food it had already consumed.
Still another region was found where stimulation
would keep the animal from eating even though it
was starving.

Such experiments soon proved beyond a doubt that
the hypothalamus was responsible for some of the
body's most vital functions. Here was the part of the
brain that controlled the appetite and also regulated
the heartbeat and blood pressure. But even more star-
tling results were still to come.

In the early 1950's a scientist named James Olds at
McGill University in Montreal, Canada, discovered
quite by accident that the hypothalamus is also the

seat of our emotions. One day, before he had quite mastered the technique of implanting electrodes, he pushed a wire a little deeper into the brain of a rat than he meant to. When he delivered a shock, Olds observed that the rat behaved very strangely. It seemed to get great pleasure from the stimulation, and it returned to the same corner of the cage where it was sitting when it got the shock, as if asking for more. Olds was quite surprised, and he devised an experi-

ment to find out whether the rat really did enjoy the shock. He rigged a lever in the cage, which the rat could press to shock itself. As soon as it learned what the lever was for, the rat started pressing it over and over again until he fell over exhausted. No one could doubt that the rat was enjoying the shocks. Olds had discovered the part of the brain that makes rats, at least, feel happy. Scientists soon came to call it "the pleasure center."

The discovery of such powerful centers in the hypothalamus made many researchers wonder whether there might not also be a "sleep center." Some evidence that the brain controls sleep had already been collected. In 1890, a Viennese eye doctor, Ludwig Mauthner, noticed strange swellings in the brains of a number of patients who had died in an epidemic of sleeping sickness. These patients had all succumbed to the major symptom of the disease, a profound, unwakable sleep. Mauthner reasoned that the swellings could have caused this symptom by pressing on a part of the brain that normally regulates sleep.

During the 1930's and 1940's, Hess, who had done the original experiments on the hypothalamus, came up with even more definite evidence that there were sleep and wakefulness centers in the brain. By moving his electrodes from place to place in the hypothalamus, he eventually found one region that would cause a sleeping animal to wake up every time it was stimulated. Not satisfied with this discovery, he kept working and soon found another region that, when stimulated, would cause an animal to fall asleep.

Other scientists began discovering more and more parts of the brain that would cause a sleeping animal to wake up. As they learned more about the structure of the brain, they discovered that all of the "wake-up centers" were located in a network of cells called the reticular (netlike) activating system. This interlocking formation of cells extends from the top of the spinal cord through the brainstem and hypothalamus up to the cerebral cortex. Scientists had long suspected that the activating system had something to do with controlling an animal's sleep. If its connections to the cerebral cortex were severed, the animal would fall into a deep sleep from which it could never be awakened although it remained alive. Therefore, the scientists reasoned, the activating system must normally be responsible for keeping an animal awake.

It was not until 1946, however, that anyone really understood how the activating system also caused a sleeping animal to wake up. This important piece of evidence was provided by two researchers at the University of California, G. Moruzzi and H. W. Magoun. They decided to see what effect stimulating the activating system had on the cerebral cortex. To find out, they put two electrodes in the cortex of a cat and hooked them up to an EEG, which made a tracing of the brain waves. Then they put a stimulating electrode in the reticular activating system. When the cat fell asleep, its brain waves became slow and regular, the typical sleeping pattern. But when the scientists stimulated the reticular activating system, the brain waves changed immediately to the rapid shallow waves that mean that a cat is awake.

Finally, the researchers understood how the reticular activating system worked. It woke up an animal by changing the pattern of the brain waves in the cerebral cortex. But like most experiments, this one did not give the whole answer. For as scientists always remember, it is one thing to make something happen in the artificial conditions of a laboratory experiment, but it is quite another to prove that this is also what happens in an animal that is leading a normal life. Moruzzi and Magoun were quick to do another experiment. This time they wanted to find out whether the activating system influenced the cortex when a cat woke up normally. First they had to find a normal way to wake up a sleeping cat. Soon they hit upon it. They could make a loud noise or flash a bright light or touch the cat's paws or pinch it. In other words, they could stimulate its sense organs. They tried all these methods and many more. The result was always the same. When they stimulated any sense organ, a current passed through the activating system, each time changing the cerebral brain waves.

There is still much that remains mysterious about the activating system. But at least in a general way scientists have come to understand how it works. By probing all its branches with tiny electrodes, they have discovered that all nerves running from sense organs to the brain have branches that lead to the activating system. This means that every time a message travels to the brain from a sense organ, it goes to the activating system. The activating system, in turn, sends a message to the cerebral cortex. No matter which sense organ has sent the original message, the activating system's message to the cortex is always the same. If the animal is asleep, it says, "wake up." If the animal is already awake, the message says, "be alert."

The activating system does more than merely alert the brain when it sends the message "wake up." It also alerts the muscles so they will be ready to accept any commands the cortex might send to them. It can even work to help you concentrate. You may have noticed that when you are reading an interesting book or playing a game outside you do not hear when someone calls you. Your activating system has tuned out the messages coming from your ears and lets you give all your attention to what you are doing.

The activating system explains how the brain wakes us up. But what makes us sleep? Hess and the researchers who continued his work found some parts of the brain that, when stimulated, caused an animal to fall

asleep. But many of these centers caused sleep only when they were stimulated with a current similar to the pattern of a sleeping animal's brain waves. Otherwise, stimulation in the same place would cause the animal to wake up. Today scientists are still not clear about how these "sleep centers" work. Possibly they tone down the influence of the activating system.

In an effort to find out what causes our pattern of sleep, scientists have turned their attention to the system of glands that control our body chemistry. Our blood is full of chemical messengers called hormones.

They are manufactured and then released into the blood stream by glands located in several parts of the body. Sleep researchers have long wondered whether the amount of one of these hormones might increase and decrease in the blood on a regular schedule and influence the brain to make us wake up and fall asleep.

There is plenty of evidence that hormones are involved in sleep. One of these chemicals, called progesterone, is made in great amounts during pregnancy and may be related to the fact that women are often uncontrollably sleepy during the first few months they are pregnant. To check the theory, researchers at the University of California Brain Research Institute tried injecting the hormone directly into the brains of cats. The animals promptly fell asleep.

The relationship between chemicals and sleep is still not at all clear, but a team of scientists at the Rockland State Hospital in Orangeburg, New York, is beginning to come up with some answers. The director of research at the hospital, Dr. Nathan S. Kline, had been experimenting with drugs to relieve a group of patients who were always depressed. Many of these patients also suffered from insomnia. One day he learned that if animals were treated first with a drug called iproniazid and then with a sedative, they became more alert and active, instead of becoming less active as they would have if treated with the sedative alone. At the same time, a physician in charge of one of the wards at Rockland State asked Kline if he knew of any drug that would help some of the patients on his ward who were depressed and apathetic. Kline suggested that he try iproniazid, and at the same time he started giving it to some of his own private patients. In both cases the patients' response was dramatic. Within a couple of weeks most of them no longer felt depressed and were able to return to a much more normal life. One thirty-year-old housewife who had suffered severe depression for seven years, and who fell back into bed as soon as her husband and children went off for the day, suddenly began to keep house efficiently and had so much energy that she started studying for a professional career.

Yet oddly enough, although the drug gave the patients much more energy, it did not increase the amount of sleep they got. In fact, it did just the opposite. The patients who had suffered insomnia got even less sleep than they had before although they did not feel at all sleepy. Somehow it made the sleep they were getting much more effective. When biochemists set to work to find out how the drug worked, they learned that it changed the chemistry of the brain. Somehow it and other drugs of its kind increased the amount of energy-giving chemicals, called amines, in the patients' brains. Later Kline found that he could make the drug work even better by giving it to patients along with a chemical-building block of the brain amines. When given the combination, patients would feel better within a few hours. Kline has suggested that someday normal people may want to take these drugs routinely to allow them to work much more efficiently. They could reduce their sleep to only two or three hours a night, and thus increase their working time by four to five hours, without feeling any fatigue.

In recent years scientists have found that two well-known hormones manufactured by the adrenal gland may play an even more important role in sleep than they had suspected. These chemicals, called noradrenalin and acetylcholine, are also manufactured by the ends of nerves in the brain and seem to carry messages from one nerve to another. Researchers have discovered that if noradrenalin is applied to the cells of the activating system, it will act just like an electric shock and cause the animal to wake up. On the other hand, if acetylcholine is applied to the cells of the "sleep centers," it causes the animal to go to sleep. In some parts of the brain, noradrenalin wakes an animal up, while acetylcholine, applied to the same spot, puts it to sleep.

Scientists still have not been able to decide which of the many chemicals are significant in the normal human cycle of sleep. Does one of them accumulate during the day and cause us to go to sleep at night? No one is sure. And until they find out, researchers will keep looking for new chemicals. Recently the French researcher Michel Jouvet, who was one of the first persons to study the effects of REM sleep, has found that still another chemical may prove to be the most important of all in regulating sleep. Working again with cats, he destroyed about 80 percent of several groups of brain cells located along the middle of the brainstem. This group of cells (called the nuclei of Raphe) is known to manufacture large amounts of serotonin, another of the brain amines. When these cells were destroyed, the cats survived, but they slept only 10 percent of the time. This was a radical change from the cats' normal pattern of sleeping away two thirds of every twenty-four hours. Jouvet continued his experiments and found that another area of the brainstem, called the locus coeruleus, seemed to be responsible specifically for bringing on REM sleep, the dreaming phase of sleep discussed in Chapter III. These cells contained large amounts of the chemical noradrenalin, which is also found in the activating system. When these cells were destroyed in a cat, the animal got no REM sleep at all. Unfortunately, the operation was so drastic that the cats also often died.

On the basis of these experiments, Jouvet has put forward a theory of sleep that goes farther than any yet proposed in explaining what makes us sleep. According to him, both the Raphe cells, which bring about light sleep, and the locus coeruleus, which brings about REM sleep, act like brakes on the reticular activating system. If the brakes were not applied, the activating system would keep us awake all the time. This does not happen, apparently because first the Raphe system brings about light sleep by manufacturing serotonin, and then the locus coeruleus brings about REM sleep by manufacturing noradrenalin. Presumably sleeping causes the brain to use up these chemicals, thus taking the brakes off the reticular activating system and allowing us to wake up again.

The relationships among all the different chemicals that affect sleep are still confusing, and a great deal more research will be necessary before anyone can be sure how they all interact with one another and with the brain's sleep and wakefulness centers. Scientists have made an exciting beginning, but the mystery still remains. Why do we sleep?

# V

# When People Go Without Sleep

We live in the strongest and richest nation in the world. The United States manufactures the most goods, grows the most food, has the highest average income per family, and boasts by far the most television sets, cars, and appliances. As a whole, Americans are the best-traveled, best-housed, and best-fed of all peoples. But they are probably the worst sleepers.

Dr. George Gallup, the famous poll-taker, discovered

this remarkable fact when he inquired into the sleeping habits of the people of eight nations—the United States, Canada, Great Britain, France, Denmark, the Netherlands, Norway, and Sweden. His survey indicated that one out of every two adult Americans has trouble sleeping. In France, one out of three experiences sleeping problems. And in the Scandinavian countries, the figure is only one out of four.

There are many kinds of sleeping difficulties—some extremely serious and others familiar to everyone. Dr. Gallup's poll investigated the familiar kind, called insomnia. A person may be said to suffer from insomnia if he finds it hard to fall asleep or if he wakes up repeatedly during the night or if he falls asleep easily but wakes up in the early hours of the morning. An occasional bout of sleeplessness is normal. The people we call insomniacs, however, experience it virtually every night.

The Gallup poll turned up a fascinating array of statistics about insomnia:

1. Married people have less insomnia than single people. The divorced and widowed have the most insomnia of all.

2. Women have more insomnia than men.

3. The middle-aged have about twice as much insomnia as those in their twenties.

4. College graduates sleep better than people with only a grammar-school education.

5. The chief cause of insomnia, according to the people interviewed, is nervous tension. This perhaps explains why Americans, a notoriously competitive and tense people, have such a high rate of insomnia.

Not everyone considers sleeplessness a bad thing. Thomas Edison, who slept only three or four hours a night (but took naps during the day), regarded the eight-hour sleep as "a heritage from cave man days." The inventor added: "Now that we've got electric lights, we may be able to change all that."

Most insomniacs find Edison's ideas about sleep very unappealing. They know what it is like to toss and turn all night while their friends and family are sound asleep. They know what misery it is to wake up groggy and irritable in the gray pre-dawn hours, longing for a few more hours of sleep with no hope of getting it. Anyone walking through the city or suburbs will see a few lights burning, no matter what time it is. In the silence of their bedrooms, the insomniacs are keeping their unwanted vigil, wishing that their minds would slip into blissful unconsciousness.

Insomniacs will try almost anything to put themselves to sleep. They may read a dull, difficult book to induce drowsiness. Some insomniacs find that exciting mystery books have the same effect. Some raid refrigerators and others purposely go to bed hungry. Some count sheep or say prayers or think through everything that happened during the day. Some drink

warm milk; others turn to liquor; many people take sleeping pills. The nineteenth-century English novelist Charles Dickens had an exceedingly strange way of bringing on sleep: whenever he was traveling or visiting a friend's house and slept in a new bedroom, he would rearrange the furniture so that the head of the bed pointed due north. This was indispensable for good sleep, Dickens believed.

Enterprising businessmen, it seems, are very much aware of the vast numbers of adults who struggle against wakefulness each night. A great many sleep-inducing gadgets are manufactured today. You can buy sleep masks, ear plugs, knee pillows, head-warmers, a variety of mechanical vibrators, and go-to-sleep records of soft music. Insomniacs with a flair for the bizarre will find on the market the Sleepy Head—a gorillalike head guaranteed to win any staring contest and stare the opponent to sleep. An especially desperate insomniac may want another, large-scale gadget—a Fiberglas tub that is meant for resting, not bathing. Mineral salts are added to the water in the tub, and the insomniac floats, just as he would in ocean water; this induces complete relaxation and, theoretically, cuts down on the need for sleep.

These devices may conceivably help. But there are simpler ways. The bedroom should be dark and quiet. The bed should be covered with enough blankets to keep the sleeper warm, because cold definitely keeps people awake. For proper comfort, the sheets should be changed fairly often, since people perspire quite a bit during sleep. Even the color of the walls in the bedroom may make a difference: bright reds and oranges tend to excite the mind, while soft shades of green and blue have a soothing effect. (The walls in many mental hospitals are painted blue or green to have this same effect on the patients.)

The bed itself is considered important. Although man can sleep almost anywhere if he has to—campers in sleeping bags, sailors in hammocks, primitive man on the ground—a medium-hard, resilient bed evidently provides the best rest.

Cold temperatures, bright lights, soft beds, and almost any kind of bodily ache or pain may bring on insomnia. But the principal villain is worry—usually worry about the sleep-loss itself. Many insomniacs are convinced that they will be mental and physical wrecks the next day if they do not get their full eight hours of sleep. They go to bed fretting, keep themselves awake and miserable by their fear of sleeplessness, and consequently have all the more reason to fret again the next night. A high proportion of insomniacs are caught in this vicious cycle. Their fear that they are not getting enough sleep keeps them awake.

One recent study has shown that the quality of the sleep insomniacs get, as well as the amount, is lower than normal. In one group of insomniacs the average pulse rate was 60.5 beats per minute when they were asleep as opposed to 56.6 beats for normal sleepers. Insomniacs' temperature, too, was higher than that of normal sleepers. This higher pulse rate and temperature seems to indicate that the bodies of insomniacs are much more active than those of normal people when they are asleep. An even clearer indication of the poor sleep that insomniacs suffer came from studying them with EEG's. Investigators found that they spent an abnormal amount of time in light sleep and that most of their deep sleep came early in the night; therefore, they were more likely to wake up in the second half of the night. Furthermore, the insomniacs got quite a bit less rapid eye movement (REM) sleep, the mysterious phase when the brain is dreaming and hyperactive. In short, the EEG records proved that insomnia entails much more than mere loss of sleep-time; it also is characterized by an abnormal distribution of the various phases of brain activity during sleep.

This indicates that insomnia and worry are related more than coincidentally. In psychological terms, poor sleepers are more anxious, introspective, and emotionally disturbed people than good sleepers are. In physiological terms, they sleep more lightly. Because insomnia and personality are so closely bound together, the appearance of sleeping problems in the life of a normally good sleeper actually serves as a warning that the person is experiencing emotional disorders and quite possibly needs a doctor's attention.

Probably not one insomniac could be found in the world who says that he enjoys not sleeping well. Yet it is a fact that a great many people in this country take pills to stay awake. Every year, eight billion of these wake-up pills—called amphetamines—are manufactured in the United States. In some cases, doctors prescribe the pills for people who have very low energy or who need to lose weight (the pills reduce appetite). But a great many people use them for the wrong reasons. Insomniacs who rely on heavy doses of go-to-sleep pills often gobble down a couple of wake-up amphetamines in the morning just to shake off their grogginess. Students facing exams and businessmen going through a grueling round of meetings often take amphetamines to keep alert during a long, tiring period. Truck drivers use the pills to enable them to drive long hauls without rest. Some teenagers recklessly take the pills by the handful because it gives them an artificial sense of exhilaration. Illegal amphetamine-selling, a business run by organized crime rings, is a five-hundred-million-dollar-per-year racket.

These pills are dangerous. They do not eliminate fatigue. They merely disguise it, cover it up, give the user a sense that he is more alert than he really is. Truck drivers who use these pills feel perfectly alert as they drive hour after hour, but in reality their reflexes are slowed down and ultimately they may suffer hallucinations from overdoses and excessive fatigue. One driver jackknifed his tractor-trailer because he was fighting off a nine-foot black snake that he *thought* he saw in the cab of the truck. Policemen know how to recognize a driver who is on amphetamines: the pupils of his eyes are larger than normal and he is nervous, giddy, and very talkative.

There are many amphetamine addicts in the United States, usually people who started to take the pill because they liked the feeling of exhilaration it gave them. At first a person will take only one or two pills at a time. But after a while one or two pills are not enough because his body has become used to the dosage. He takes three or four, then more, to achieve the desired effect. As one Oklahoma amphetamine ad-

dict told the police: "I started taking just one pill at a time and got a kick, and then one wasn't enough, until I was taking a jarful [one thousand tablets] every week. I saw some of these guys who'd take a couple of handfuls and swallow them down one at a time." The addict gradually begins to lose his appetite. As his dosage grows large, he begins to act partially insane. If he is lucky, he will end up in a hospital in time to break the habit. If he is unlucky, his brain may become permanently damaged.

Pills that interfere with sleep are quite obviously dangerous. And loss of sleep because of insomnia is obviously unpleasant. It does not seem likely, then, that anyone would ever want to do without sleep altogether. But the fact is, a few sometimes do. People occasionally do go on "wakathons," sometimes as a scientific experiment and sometimes as a publicity stunt. But for whatever reason people deprive themselves of sleep, one thing becomes dramatically clear: going without sleep is just as perilous as going without food.

The record for sleeplessness is held by a San Diego high school student. He stayed awake for a little more than eleven days and nights. Recently, Rick Michaels, a twenty-seven-year-old disk-jockey for station WBRB in Roseville, Michigan, tried to beat that record. To publicize a charity, he set out to stay awake for as long as his body could stand it. Using no stimulants except coffee, he lasted ten days. It was unquestionably the worst ordeal of his life.

For the first three days the disk-jockey actually enjoyed himself. It was a new and interesting experience, and it did not seem to affect his health in any way. During the early hours of each morning he had to struggle to keep his eyes open; but when he took a brisk walk and stepped under a shower, he felt wide awake again.

After the third day Michaels grew more and more irritable. When a woman offered him a bowl of soup, he refused to eat and accused her of trying to over-protect him. At one point an observer squeezed his nose to keep him awake, and the disk-jockey screamed, "You're all trying to make a fool out of me, and I'm quitting." He did not quit, however, and his mood soon changed.

After one hundred hours he began to talk in an excited, boastful way, describing how he was easily going to break the "wakathon" record. "Now you'll see the real Rick Michaels. I'm giving up all that artificial stuff and just behave like myself. I'm not worried about it anymore. I'm sure of it now." He ate a gigantic meal, and chattered on and on.

When he had been awake for one hundred and sixty hours, a new Rick Michaels appeared. He now looked like a man who was as weary as a human being could possibly be. His brow was furrowed in worry, and he complained of "tightness and dryness" in his joints and "great heaviness" of his hands and feet. He began to have hallucinations, as if he were dreaming while he was wide awake. He saw "a gray mist hanging . . . like a spider web." A woman came into the room and gave him some coffee, and she seemed surrounded in blue flame. Then the imaginary flame spurted out of the wall and drove him from the room in terror. He also seemed full of a sense of persecution: once he grabbed a companion by the throat and started to choke him because he thought the man was trying to make fun of him.

Gradually, the disk-jockey lost all his powers of concentration. He would forget what he had done only moments before. The slightest noise distracted his thoughts. The simplest tasks seemed extremely difficult to him. Periodically he would withdraw into sullen silence. Hallucinations like the blue flame plagued him continually. He felt a tight band around his head, and the imaginary band slowly slipped down over his eyes and made it difficult to see.

At 220 hours, Michaels could barely talk and had to be held up when he walked. At noontime, 243 hours after his ordeal had begun, he went to sleep while standing up, falling into the arms of his attendants. After fourteen hours of sleep, he awoke refreshed and feeling normal.

Rick Michaels' symptoms—irritability, followed by

hallucinations and lapses of concentration—were typical of all such "wakathons." Complete absence of sleep brings on changes in personality that resemble insanity. (One disk-jockey, in fact, ended up in a mental institution after going without sleep for a long period.)

During the middle ages in Europe, people were sometimes accused of practicing witchcraft. One of the ways of torturing them was to prevent them from going to sleep. Many of these "witches" were, in fact, mentally ill, and the enforced sleeplessness not only failed to drive the witchcraft out of them but drove them deeper and deeper into insanity.

A time-proven way of getting a confession of guilt from someone is to keep him awake for a long time. This method was used on American prisoners by the Chinese communists during the Korean War. It was called brainwashing. The prisoners were awakened at frequent intervals during the night and were bombarded with questions about how the Americans were practicing germ warfare, which was, of course, absolutely untrue. But as sleep-loss mounted, the prisoners became confused about time, lost their ability to concentrate, and sometimes began to believe that they actually had dropped germ bombs on Korea.

The record for sleeplessness, as mentioned earlier, is a little more than eleven days and nights, or 268 hours. Beyond this limit, the human body and mind seem to rebel and simply cannot be kept awake. A group of rats in a laboratory experiment surpassed the human record, however. Young rats were placed on a water wheel that was slowly rotating. If the rats fell asleep, they would drop into the water. To the astonishment of the men conducting the experiment, some of the rats walked forward on the wheel for twenty-seven days without once dropping into the water. Were

they awake all this time? No. EEG tests showed that they were running forward on the wheel, then snatching about ten seconds of sleep as the wheel carried them backward toward the water, and at the last moment waking up and running forward again. But even as the rats went through this amazing feat of endurance, they were probably suffering something equivalent to the horrors that Rick Michaels, the disk-jockey, experienced when he stayed awake for 243 hours.

How much sleep do we need? There is probably no single answer. The need for sleep varies greatly from person to person, culture to culture, age group to age group. The popular theory that everybody needs at least eight hours sleep per night has no scientific basis. Most people get between six and nine hours, but one hard-working man in Baltimore supposedly gets along on only one hour of sleep each night. On the other hand, many perfectly healthy people are accustomed to sleeping at least ten hours each night.

Campaigning politicians, soldiers at war, and harried businessmen often have to narrow down their sleeping time to five or six hours, and they usually can do it without any damage to their health. Frequently, these people take brief naps during the day to make up for some of the lost sleep. When Winston Churchill was prime minister of Great Britain during the second world war, he always napped for one hour in the early afternoon. Presidents Harry S Truman and Lyndon Johnson also have made a practice of napping during the day to conserve energy.

Many people divide their sleep, hoping to work more efficiently. Students approaching exams sometimes take two long naps of three hours each rather than sleep six hours straight. One businessman trained himself to sleep for a half hour every three hours (getting a total of four hours of sleep a day); he kept to this routine for two years without any ill effects, but he finally gave it up because it interfered with his social life. Usually we assume that the millions of night workers in the world sleep straight through the day. This is not so. Most night workers go home at eight o'clock in the morning, eat breakfast, sleep until about one o'clock, get up for lunch and play with the children, then go back to sleep.

The practice of napping or dividing sleep is very common in the animal kingdom, scientists have noted. White rats in laboratories take ten "rest periods" each day. Rabbits take sixteen to twenty-one of these daily naps, and even earthworms rest four times during each twenty-four-hour period. The sleep of some animals, however, is more like drowsiness than deep slumber.

In general, animals in their natural surroundings spend about two thirds of their lives sleeping or dozing and more if they are of the hibernating type. The human infant, for the first three months of life, also sleeps about two thirds of the time. But as the child grows, he begins to need less and less sleep. By his late teens, sleep-time is generally down to about eight hours. Older people often sleep less and tend to wake up during the night.

Wakefulness is important in the modern world. Life offers more entertainment, more social companionship, and more comfort than ever before in history. Some scientists—although their opinions are controversial—believe that there is actually a trend toward less sleep in response to the high value of wakefulness in the modern world. Dr. Mangalore Pai, a British authority on sleep, says:

*There is much more to do nowadays, more reason to stay awake. The cave man slept during all the hours of darkness. He even slept during the daytime if he had nothing else to do. That is exactly what people in backward countries do, even now. I have studied Indian villages where the only lights are paraffin lamps. The natives sleep nine, ten, eleven hours a night. Tell one of them to sleep only seven hours, and he feels all sorts of symptoms. Yet when the same man goes to a city, he cuts down his sleep and stays awake to see the lights, the sights, the cinema. It is a part of man's evolutionary process that he should sleep less and less as he discovers more reasons for staying awake.*

*All around us, a great evolutionary change is taking*

*place in the world, and I am convinced that having fewer hours of sleep is one of its aspects. Children today are stronger; they are more capable of endurance; they mature earlier; their brains are more active; they are restless in their pursuit of knowledge. There is a continuous upsurge in mental and physical activity and in the sources that stimulate visual perception—television, movies, reading. It is inevitable that physiological changes should follow. Reduction in hours of sleep is one of them. It's a sign of good health.*

# VI

# The Frontiers of Research
# on Sleep

Science is explaining and changing our world at an
extraordinary pace. A hundred years ago, many people
thought that all the problems had been solved and
all the inventions invented. But with every year that
passes, new stars are discovered, rockets probe farther
into space, new drugs are devised to combat disease,
physicists explore the invisible innards of the atom,
electronic devices like Telstar satellites and infrared
ovens alter our existence, and more is learned about

the world. This avalanche of knowledge is accelerating. Every week almost two billion words are written about science and technology; even if a person could read eight hours a day for a full lifetime, he still could not finish reading the material about one week's scientific exploration. No one person can keep up with all these advances. On the other hand, nobody seriously expects the scientific revolution to stop, and few people want it to.

Where does sleep fit in this revolution? The study of sleep is, in fact, a champion example of the explosion of scientific knowledge. Before this century, almost nothing accurate was known about the mysterious third of our lives spent in sleep. Folklore about sleep has never revealed much. People still say, "He slept like a log," meaning the person hardly moved after he went to bed, yet scientists now know that every normal person awakens several times a night (although he may not remember it) and that most people stir or change position twenty to sixty times during eight hours of sleep. Another saying is, "He slept like a baby," meaning his sleep was deep and steady. Yet a recent study of the sleep of new-born infants indicated that their longest average period of continuous sleep was only about four hours. Clearly, folk-sayings and tradition do not provide us with much accurate information about sleep.

Science is making up for lost time. There are now

two dozen or more sleep laboratories in this country. The army, navy, and air force all have research programs investigating sleep. The United States space program is exceedingly interested in sleep because astronauts of the future will have no night or day to tell them when to rest. Knowledge about sleep is pouring out of these laboratories and may someday change our lives.

First and foremost, scientists want to know how sleep works. But they have other practical goals as well. Many scientists think that our sleeping habits can be changed or controlled, and programs are now investigating ways of inducing sleep with harmless drugs, with electronic devices, and—most dramatic of all—by mental control. Another important line of research aims at curing some of the more severe abnormalities of sleep.

One is bed-wetting. About 2 percent of the adult population suffers from this problem. Until recently, most doctors thought that bed-wetting was caused by dreams. But in a recent EEG study of children, it was found that bed-wetting occurred not in the REM dreaming phase of sleep but in a deeper stage. Having discovered this, doctors tried a special drug on children that lightens their sleep so that they can wake up easily when they have to go to the bathroom. This drug does prevent bed-wetting, but unfortunately it produces a side-effect of irritability during the day. More research will have to be done.

Another common abnormality of sleep is sleepwalking, or somnambulism. Around four million Americans are affected with this problem. Sleepwalkers can perform some remarkable feats while remaining completely unconscious. One investigator reported the case of a college student who formed the habit of getting up in his sleep, dressing, and walking three quarters of a mile to a river, going for a swim, and then returning to his bed. Another reported a man who walked along a ledge of windows twelve stories high without waking up. Perhaps the most bizarre example of all was the experience of a whole family of sleepwalkers: one night, father, mother, and the four children got up at three in the morning and gathered around their tea table. Only when one of the children knocked over a chair did they wake up.

It had long been thought that sleepwalking was in some way related to dreaming, but a recent study shows that it is not. Four investigators at the University of California studied a group of nine sleepwalkers ranging in age from nine years old to twenty-three. Using the EEG, they traced the subjects brainwaves throughout the night to determine in what phase of sleep sleepwalking occurred. They hooked the subjects to the machine with long cords so that they would have plenty of room to move around if they should get out of bed. Instead of finding that the subjects walked during the REM or dreaming phase of sleep, the investigators were surprised to discover that all sleepwalking

activity occurred in the deep phase of sleep. There-fore, they concluded that, as with bed-wetting, there is little possibility that sleepwalking is related in any way to dreaming. Again, the subject needs more re-search.

People in the modern world use drugs in thousands of ways: for example, to relieve headaches, to cure disease, and to lose weight. Drug-manufacturing is one of the biggest businesses in the United States. Many drugs relate to sleep. In some cases they are used against afflictions like bed-wetting, but more often they serve to switch on and off the sleep of fairly normal people.

Almost everyone knows that some drugs can induce sleep. The first truly effective sleeping pills were made in 1903 by a German chemist, Emil Fischer, and were given the name barbiturates. In the fifty years that followed, a great many pharmaceutical products of varying strengths were built on the basic chemical formula for barbiturates, and the manufacture of these pills is now a multimillion-dollar enterprise. Doctors prescribe the pills for about twenty million patients each year and occasionally prescribe them very carelessly. Barbiturates can be highly dangerous. In the first place, the body gets used to them, and a person often begins to take larger and larger doses to get the same effect. Many people become addicted to the drugs (there are at least one million known barbiturate addicts in this country). When the daily intake grows beyond one or two grams, the user begins to slur his words, as if he were drunk; he shows confusion, disorientation, and sometimes symptoms that resemble insanity. He may end up in a coma—or worse. Each year thousands of people commit suicide by taking a bottleful of barbiturates. And sometimes death comes by accident: if a person takes a few sleeping pills after he has been drinking alcoholic beverages, the combination of the two may cause his heart to stop. Death is sometimes caused by the shock of taking a barbiturate addict off the pills too quickly rather than cutting down his dosage gradually.

In the 1950's, a new class of drugs was discovered to have sleep-inducing powers. These drugs were given the name tranquilizers. Where barbiturates seem to bring on sleep by acting on portions of the brain that are involved in thinking, tranquilizers work by reducing tension and anxiety. These pills, too, possess some unfortunate properties. Like barbiturates, they seem to reduce the amount of REM sleep that a person gets during the night if they are taken in large doses. Also, the pills can be habit-forming. In fact, it can be said that no sleep-inducing drug—either barbiturates, tranquilizers, or any other—has been invented that does not pose some danger of addiction or overdose. But many doctors are certain that a perfectly safe sleeping pill will someday be found, and much research is being done in the hope of finding it soon.

Drugs are not the only way of inducing sleep. For years scientists have been investigating the possibility of putting people to sleep with electricity. Russian scientists have experimented extensively with devices that pulse a very mild electrical current into the brain through electrodes attached behind the ears and at the nape of the neck. Such devices seem to work well with animals. At the University of California in Los Angeles, experimenters have put cats to sleep by electrical stimulation of the brain, even while the cats were stalking a rat. Unfortunately, no instrument has been built that will put human beings to sleep as efficiently. The sleep of animals is evidently much easier to control. Frogs, guinea pigs, cats, and dogs sometimes can be coaxed into a drowsy state simply by slow caresses. If you stroke the animal gently for a few minutes and close its eyes, it will become very relaxed. Then, if you lift its eyelids, you will see that the animal is in a sleeping state because its eyeballs are rolled upward and the pupils are dilated, or enlarged.

Just as gentle caressing brings on drowsiness in animals, activity involving certain kinds of rhythm makes humans sleepy. Counting sheep is an example of rhythmical stimulation, and it works for many people. A British psychiatrist recently did a study in which he periodically flashed a light in the eyes of his subject and at the same time gave him an electric shock and triggered a loud booming sound. You might think that all this would only make a person more wide awake. But in this experiment, the rhythmical quality of the disturbances quickly induced sleep, even in a man who had recently awakened from a full night's sleep.

The quest for a way to bring on sleep probably

dates all the way back to the first case of insomnia. Today, science is pouring large quantities of research money and time into projects to learn how to artificially induce sleep by harmless drugs, electrical machines, and so forth. Almost everyone has sought his own solution to the problem of bringing on sleep: he tries leaving the window open at night; he tries a different number of blankets; he tries sleeping with pillows and without pillows. The most desirable solution of all would be to learn how to go to sleep not by artificial, mechanical inducements but simply by mental control. If people could achieve this, it would be of tremendous benefit for all of humanity, not just for insomniacs. If a person could doze off at any time during the day by some sort of mental control like counting sheep, he would be able to use his time far more efficiently than is presently possible. A businessman could sleep between appointments; a housewife could catch a few moments of rest while she was waiting for a meal to cook; a student could snatch sleep between classes.

Is it a dream to hope that people can learn to go to sleep—at any time during the day—by mental control? Many sleep experts give a qualified no. Recent experiments have proved that ordinary people are capable of acquiring control over a drowsy preliminary stage of sleep—called the alpha state—that shows up as slow, regular brain waves on the EEG. One investigator

trained a group of subjects to switch on alpha rhythm at will. First he taught them to recognize the state by ringing a bell and then asking them to tell him whether they were in alpha rhythm or not. He checked by monitoring their brain waves with an EEG. Quickly they learned to tell, and soon after that they learned to bring on the state themselves, although they were not exactly sure how they did it.

Sleep experts are not sure where such research will lead. They note that the alpha-wave state is really a level of consciousness that lies somewhere between sleep and wakefulness. It is not true sleep, nor can it replace sleep, but it is very restful. It proves that some degree of mental control of sleep lies within the power of every person. Perhaps people will never be able to switch on and off the deeper phases of sleep, but scientists do not rule out the possibility. The age-old habit of sleeping through the night may someday disappear, although not in the near future. Most experts believe that we are going to change many of our ideas about when a person should sleep. "If you were born in an eighteen-hour world or a twenty-seven-hour world," one pioneering sleep-scientist says, "you would operate just as well as in a twenty-four-hour world." If we learn to rest ourselves periodically by mentally inducing the lighter phases of sleep, we may greatly extend the length of time that we can go without deep sleep. If such an ability is eventually developed, it will change our world.

Countless unlikely materials have become valuable resources in the modern world: chemists have learned how to make thousands of products, ranging from drugs to nylon, out of the black material called coal; engineers extract valuable minerals like magnesium from common sea-water; high-protein food is being concocted from ground-up fish. The list could yet go on and on. In this age almost everything is exploited. Why then, many people have asked, should we throw away one third of our lives in sleep? There are never enough hours in the day, these people complain. It is true, they admit, that no one can stop sleeping altogether, but they wish that the sleep itself could be put to use.

Amazingly enough, science is trying. People who are asleep certainly cannot do manual labor. But a few scientists suspect that people can use sleep as a time for learning and thinking. If the mind could be put to work during the hours of night, students could educate themselves far more quickly, a busy housewife might be able to pick up several foreign languages, and all of us might find ourselves spouting facts in the daytime that we would not remember learning because we had learned them when we were asleep. Should we continue to sleep in silence as mankind always has, or should we play tape-recorded lessons during the night? The majority of sleep experts think that we should forget about sleep-learning and sleep-thinking. But there is some fairly persuasive evidence for trying it.

In the first place, we know that people are not totally shut off from the world while they are asleep. A cold breeze, a pressure, or a sharp noise will wake anyone up. Furthermore, a certain amount of discrimination between sensations goes on: a mother will awaken to her baby's cry but not to the sound of a passing truck; a hunter wakes up at the sound of a cracking twig but is not bothered by the hoot of an owl.

These examples are obvious. Few people know, however, that it is possible to solve problems during sleep. The mathematician John von Neumann, one of the men who developed computers, wrote complex equations in his sleep. A well-known neurophysiologist at the Massachusetts Institute of Technology, Warren McCulloch, solves problems during the night that baffle him when he is awake. Another professor from MIT, the famous mathematician Norbert Wiener, used to go to sleep during meetings with his scientific colleagues. "He'd be snoring," says a friend, "he'd snore in your face as you talked, but if you made a mistake, he would wake up and correct you."

Some people, then, can think during sleep. This is a very exciting idea, one that seems to offer great opportunities, in the opinion of many businessmen. Since the first world war, a multimillion-dollar industry based on sleep-teaching devices has grown up. Throughout the United States, companies are promoting programs said to be able to teach—during sleep—such far-ranging things as foreign languages, engineering, personality improvement, and how to give up smoking and nail-biting. Usually, the sleep-teaching machines are tape-recorders or record-players that repeat a message over and over into the ear of the sleeper. For example, an instruction course in Italian offers an under-the-pillow speaker connected to a record-player; at night, an automatic clock attachment periodically switches on the record, which supposedly helps the student memorize the words.

Two scientists investigated such sleep-teaching programs at length during the 1950's. They decided that it was possible to do some teaching during the light

Stage 1 phase of sleep but that learning was not possible during the deeper stages. There is disagreement, however. A leading army hospital did an experiment using electric shocks and flashing lights to wake up volunteers during the night; the experimenters found that the volunteers learned to press a button that would shut off the shocks and lights even when they were in deep sleep. The Russians are hard at work on sleep-teaching studies. One study reports that Russian youths learned a vocabulary of one thousand English words in just twenty-two nights of training.

Thus, the subject is still open. Perhaps someday the "lost" third of our lives will be put to productive use. Like other studies that are pushing against the frontiers of our knowledge about sleep—searching for drugs that can harmlessly induce sleep, searching for the mental mechanisms that might enable us to control sleep—there is reason to hope that sleep-learning will be a fruitful line of research. Meanwhile, science is going ahead as fast as it can, exploring this mysterious, complex state called sleep. No one can say what gifts to humanity this research will yield, but the gifts may be great indeed.

Students of sleep find themselves in a situation familiar to all scientists: the more they learn, the more questions seem to arise. For instance, cells were once thought to be fairly simple building-blocks of living material; but as microscopes have enabled scientists to look closer, cells are seen to be extremely complex mechanisms that perform a great many chemical functions—some of which are still not understood. Similarly with sleep, the closer we look, the more complex it all seems.

We make our strange journey up and down through layers of consciousness every night, and thousands of EEG studies by scientists have charted the way clearly. But, although we are quite familiar with the brain-wave shifts, we still do not really know what the brain is doing. When REM sleep was discovered during the 1950's, many people began to hope that the strange, sometimes beautiful, sometimes horrible world of dreams would soon be thoroughly explored. The EEG showed that every normal person enters the dreaming state approximately every ninety minutes during the night, but it told us nothing about the meaning of dreams. Many scientific experiments are currently exploring this question of meaning, but their task is enormously complicated because the dreams of each individual are based on his personal storehouse of memories. Even psychiatrists, who spend years learning about the past of their patients, admit that they cannot correctly interpret dreams more than 50 percent of the time. One thing we do know about dreams, however: we must have them. Drugs, alcohol, and loss of sleep all interfere with dreaming and can cause hallucinations and other effects that resemble insanity.

Just as the EEG cannot penetrate the meaning of dreams, so it cannot disclose the cause of sleep. It is in the area of the biochemical nature of sleep that most research remains to be done. The chemicals that determine bodily behavior are very difficult to isolate. Scientists suspect that the body produces quite a few sleep-inducing substances. Perhaps someday drug manufacturers will be supplying us with two simple pills that will switch these master chemicals on and off, giving us a natural, nonaddictive means of controlling our sleep. That day seems to be far off, however.

Summing it up, what do we know? We know that the reticular activating system is crucial in switching sleep on and off. From the EEG we know the strange electrical behavior of the brain as it dips down into unconsciousness and gropes back toward alertness. We do not know the chemical behavior of the brain, but we are learning more about it. If we are ever to understand sleep, we must closely examine this chemistry. We do not know very much about dreams, and probably dreams will never be measured by scientific instruments as other functions of the body can be. All in all, we know far more about sleep than mankind did fifty years ago, but much is still a mystery. Yet every night, as darkness settles on the earth, and billions of people retire to their beds, a few volunteers are entering scientific laboratories to get their sleep. Under the watchful eye of scientists and the even more acute eye of devices like the EEG, these volunteers are donating their sleep to the cause of knowledge. There is still much that we do not know—but we are learning.